RIDGES and VALLEYS

Walks in the Midlands

by
Trevor A

Meridian Books

Published 1992 by Meridian Books
Reprinted 1993 (with amendments)

© Trevor Antill 1992

ISBN 1-869922-15-8

A catalogue record for this book is available from the British Library.

The right of Trevor Antill to be identified as the author of this work has been asserted by him in accordance with the Copyright, Designs and Patents Act 1988.

Publishers' Note

Every care has been taken in the preparation of this book. All the walks have been independently checked and are believed to be correct at the time of publication. However, neither the author nor the publishers can accept responsibility for any errors or omissions or for any loss, damage, injury or inconvenience resulting from the use of the book.

Please remember that the countryside is continually changing: hedges and fences may be removed or re-sited; landmarks may disappear; footpaths may be re-routed or be ploughed over and not reinstated (as the law requires); concessionary paths may be closed. The publishers would be very pleased to have details of any such changes that are observed by readers.

Also by Trevor Antill:
Ridges and Valleys II: More Walks in the Midlands
The Navigation Way: A Hundred Mile Towpath Walk (*with Peter Groves*)

Meridian Books
40 Hadzor Road, Oldbury, Warley, West Midlands B68 9LA

Printed in Great Britain by BPCC Wheatons Ltd., Exeter.

Contents

Location Map

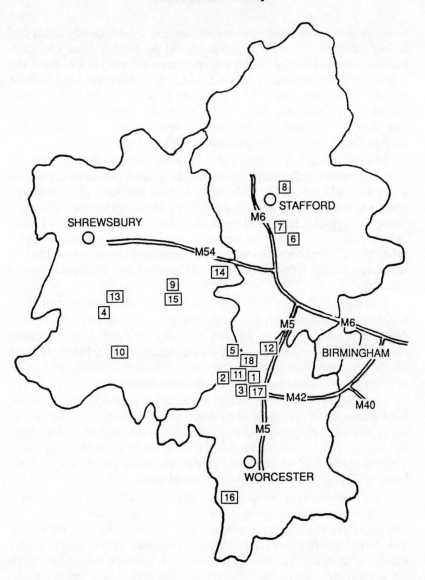

Introduction

Some people believe the countryside around the Midlands is flat and uninteresting — in reality, nothing could be further from the truth. Nothing on the scale of the Alps of course, or indeed some of the better known ridges and escarpments in Great Britain. No great heights these; but then one only needs to rise a very modest height to gain quite outstanding views, and the Midlands are no exception to this general rule. In the final analysis, no matter where you are, clear visibility is always the prerequisite for panoramic views, of any terrain!

The following is a selection of ridge and valley walks, some taking in better known hills; some lesser; but most with one or two pleasant surprises. All the walks contain other items of interest and some have a clue as to the best time to walk them. They are all within the counties of Shropshire, Staffordshire and the old county of Worcestershire — I really can't reconcile myself to that 'shot gun' wedding brought about in 1974 when two ancient counties, with little in common, were forced into that unlikely alliance called the County of Hereford and Worcester. What a mouthful!

Those of us who live in the urban parts of the Midlands, and the Black Country in particular, tend to complain of the lack of green spaces and fresh air available to us, yet, not only do we have much beautiful countryside on our borders — we are most conveniently placed to reach all the favoured places throughout Great Britain. Not many areas of the country have such a comprehensive infrastructure.

But enough of that: these walks are for those of you living a busy life where time is at a premium. Not everyone has the time — or disposition — to pore over maps and work out a likely walk, then to find it's been obliterated or obstructed! Yet most people are in need of the spiritual uplift that many of us get from a day in the country and these walks, I trust, will help achieve that happy state of mind.

On a practical note; although the following walks each have a sketch map it is strongly recommended that you also take the relevant Ordnance Survey map and, yes, even a compass. More importantly if you don't already know how — learn to use them. Way-marking is very erratic — from overkill to absolute zero — but where it does exist most organisations have adopted the Countryside Commissions recommended colour coding of yellow for public footpaths and blue for bridleways. Farmers, when they bother, have a tendency to use any material that happens to be available or lying around at the time! Public bodies, such as County Councils and the Forestry Commission, frequently create 'nature trails' which is most commendable. But why do they have such a penchant for so many different colours to indicate the grade or distance of a walk? It can be very confusing when yellow and blue marks are used indiscriminately.

The 'Countryside Access Charter', issued by the Countryside Commission, is a useful and conveniently sized publication outlining your rights and responsibilities in the countryside — it's also waterproof! Whilst most people are familiar with the Country Code I particularly like the following guide lines which seem to have a special appeal to children. You can't catch 'em too young!

- Take nothing but photographs
- Leave nothing but footprints
- Pick nothing but your way
- Kill nothing but time
- Keep nothing but memories

Above all, remember the countryside is a living and working environment that constantly changes — even the most familiar walk can look entirely different from one season to another. Whilst every effort has been made to ensure accuracy, be prepared for the occasional diversion or even obstruction. Wilful, and thereby illegal, public path obstructions should be reported to the appropriate County Council and The Ramblers Association.

Enjoy your walk, enjoy your views and may the sun shine for you.

Trevor Antill

Transport

All the walks in this book are circular and should present no problems of access to motorists. Also, with two exceptions, they can be reached by public transport, although in a few cases this involves some extra walking. Details are given in the introductory boxes to each walk. Because of the variability of services you should always check on times before setting out. Some useful telephone numbers are:

British Rail (Birmingham): 021-643 2711

Bus Services: Hereford & Worcester, 0905-766800;
Shropshire, 0345-056 785;
Staffordshire, 0785-223344;
West Midlands, 021-200 2700

About the Author

Born and educated in Walsall, the author is a qualified Banker by profession and a keen walker by inclination. Married with four children and a grandson he completed most of his National Service in Malta —

an experience which finally convinced him that Great Britain was the original 'green and pleasant land'. Since that time his outdoor interest has widened from following walks to devising them and finally recording them. Several have been published in *Country Walking* magazine and in a local evening newspaper — this is his first book of collected walks.

With many years experience of the outdoors and with more than a passing interest in the protection of the countryside, he enjoys all types of walking ranging from a short Sunday afternoon stroll to long distance backpacking expeditions. He has walked most of the long distance footpaths in Britain and has recently been engaged as a part-time Swiss guide!

"...WALK A DAY, LIVE A WEEK..."
Old French proverb

1
Nursery Slopes
Blakedown

If I had to choose a ramble suitable for introducing children to the joys of walking, this would probably be it. Maintaining children's interest and enthusiasm is of paramount importance and this circular walk has most of the ingredients necessary for that. Firstly it's short — three miles; it has water and ducks, trees a-plenty, horses, sand and even donkeys! What more could you ask for — an ice cream? Even that's possible during the summer months!

DISTANCE: 3 miles
MAPS: Landranger (1:50,000) 139
Pathfinder (1:25,000) 953
PARKING: Lay-bys in Sandy Lane
PUBLIC TRANSPORT: Midland Red services 192/292/193 to Blakedown — alight at 'The Old House at Home'. British Rail, Blakedown. See box on p. 3
START/FINISH: Sandy Lane, Blakedown (GR 880777)

PARKING beneath a large oak tree on the roadside edge of Sandy Lane, make your way back in a generally easterly direction for a few yards to pass a public footpath sign on the left — which you ignore — and then shortly reach another on the right. Go right with this second footpath sign and walk up to pass left of a coppice and then descend to a stile in a field. Cross the stile and follow the left hand fence down to a solitary oak tree where you meet a cross track. Here you have a stile in front of you and one to your left, next to a gate across the track. Cross the left hand one and follow the sandy track to a lane. Turn left

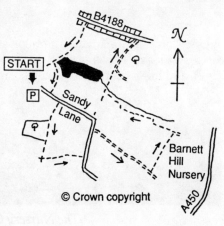

© Crown copyright

1

along the lane to arrive at a bridleway sign on the right just before a house on a left bend.

Turning right, follow the wide bridleway up to the top of Barnett Hill ridge where good views can be seen on both sides. The ridge levels out for a while and just before it widens you will come to a stile on the right. Pass this and in only a few yards you will see a stile on the left — and maybe the donkeys! Cross the left hand stile and follow the path as it gradually descends between a hedge and fence behind Barnett Hill Nurseries. Arriving at a stile cross it and join the path that crosses in front of you. If you need that ice cream you can make a short diversion right to the A450 and the garden centre shop. If not, turn left along the path following it below a field edge (left) and above a wooded dell (right) to then arrive at a gate into a field.

From here older maps show the path going diagonally left across the fields to meet Sandy Lane at Hunters Lodge. It was however diverted in November 1986 and now follows a better route which is now described.

Go through the gate and into the field where you turn right to walk the short way to the bottom corner. Here turn left, and with the fence on your right, follow it to a gate into another field. Cross this second field

The Nursery Class?

on the same line to meet another gate which takes you along a path between trees (right) and a field (left) to then meet a crossing bridleway.

At the junction with the bridleway go right, through the hunter's gate, and enter the damp woodland. Cross a culverted stream and then soon emerge in the corner of a large field. Now follow the clear path along the right hand field edge to soon join a track coming in from the right and so continue forward to head for the houses and the B4188.

Joining the road turn left along the pavement to follow it for about 500 yards, passing New House Farm, until you see a public bridleway sign on the left.

Public Transport

From The Old House at Home, Blakedown go east along the Belbroughton Road, B4188 to reach a public bridleway sign between houses numbered 52 and 54 on the right. Then pick up the route from below.

Follow the bridleway between the houses (numbers 52 and 54) to then follow the fenced way across a field to meet the corner of Ladies Pool and the ducks! Continue forward to follow the head of the pool to a point where the main track leaves the pool to go slightly right and up. Here a good path goes left to follow the pool for a short way and then join a fence above. Keeping the fence on your right follow it forward to merge with another path coming in from the left. Stay with the fence on your right and continue following it back to Sandy Lane and the start.

2
A Woodland Refuge

Wyre Forest

Although the Wyre Forest has a significant sprinkling of ubiquitous conifers, it is largely a broad-leaf forest that provides more than 6000 acres of cover for its deer herds. In part it has been designated a National Nature Reserve and this short walk, passing as it does through substantial mature oak woodlands, amply demonstrates its importance to the environment and as a refuge for man and beast. The general area — along with the River Severn and Georgian, elegant Bewdley — is so important to the Midlands that it really warrants a greater degree of protection to safeguard it from indiscriminate development.

DISTANCE: 4 miles
MAPS: Landranger (1:50,000) 138
Pathfinder (1:25,000) 952
PARKING: Off road near Callow Hill Chapel
PUBLIC TRANSPORT: Midland Red West service 192/292
(Birmingham/Kidderminster/Hereford). Alight at The Royal Forester
which is almost opposite Callow Hill Chapel.
START/FINISH: Callow Hill (GR 744739)

STARTING near Callow Hill Chapel walk west along the A456 for about 140 yards to a milestone (on the right). Almost opposite is a sign for Barncroft Nurseries and you now go left along the lane signed for the nursery car park. Passing the car park entrance stay with the lane until reaching the last house where the tarmac ends. Now continue straight ahead on a grassy track to cross a fence stile into woodland. Here your path continues forward along the woodland edge where you walk down through the oak trees to reach and cross a fence stile into a field.

In the field follow the left hedge up as it becomes a garden boundary and just before the protruding corner you will see an ornamental lamp post and a stile onto the drive. Here you ignore the stile and instead turn right to cross the centre of the field to a plank footbridge and the remains of a stile left of an oak tree. In the next field turn right to the corner and

4

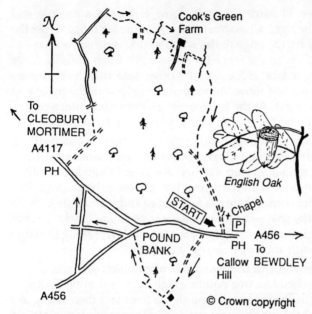

then left to walk between the field edge and the woodland. In about 100 yards, and at the second wooden pole from the corner, go right a few yards to another plank footbridge and a stile into Woodward's Coppice. In the coppice immediately join a path and go left with it to then swing right as it begins a gradual ascent. Soon the path is accompanied by a right hand fence and then merges with a track coming in from the right. Here you continue forward on the same line to then leave the woodland and enter a hedged green lane. This will soon bring you to a gate and stile onto the A456 again.

Cross over the road to go left on the pavement and then first right along the lane signed for Buckeridge. Follow this lane to crossroads and then turn right — signed Far Forest — to meet the A4117 at a T-junction. Cross the road to the pavement opposite and go left as far as the Plough Inn. Opposite the inn is a minor surfaced lane with a footpath sign at its entrance. Turn right to follow the lane for a quarter of a mile where on the left, and next to 'Cleestones', there is a white cottage with a horseshoe over its wooden porch. Immediately right of the cottage is a fence stile onto a fenced path which goes along the side of the garden. Follow it to another stile which takes you into a field where you now follow the right hand hedge to the corner where another stile and a footpath sign await you.

Over this stile you join a lane corner to then go forward on the tarmac of Sugars Lane. Passing the restored Sugars Farm on the way, you follow this lane for a little under half a mile to a junction. The left turn has a sign stating that it is a private road. You need the right fork however where in a further 50 yards you will come to a gate, step stile and footpath sign on the right. Cross over and follow the left fence across the field to a step stile on the edge of the woodland. Over this you have to go immediately left with the fence for a few yards to an unusual fence stile incorporating a footbridge. On the other side turn immediately right up a short bank to follow the edge of the field with the fence and woodland on your right. At the field corner go through a gate, next to a small corrugated metal barn, which takes you onto a farm track.

Follow the farm track for about 30 yards where there is a step stile in the fence on the left. Go over it to now follow the right hand fence for 25 yards where there is another step stile to cross. Over this go left to follow the same fence but now with it on your left. Descend the sloping field where in the bottom corner there is a footbridge and then a stile into the woodland. Cross the stile — again you have to go immediately left, but this time in 10 yards turn right with the fence to follow it along the edge of the woodland with another fence on your left.

In a short while you will come to a stile over which, just ahead, you will see a sign attached to a tree pointing right and indicating Footpath 17. Go right with the broad path through the trees and then swing left with it, passing right of sundry caravans, to meet a crossing vehicle track. Go straight across where another sign indicates your way forward on Footpath 17 through the trees to shortly arrive at a step stile onto an unsurfaced track. Joining the broad track go left to a corner — on the left is the old stile, pre-diversion — and then right around the bend to a stile at the side of a gate across what is now a hedged, fenced and unsurfaced lane. Following this lane soon descend to a stream where, if required, there is a footbridge slightly left.

On the other side of the stream you are faced with a divergence of tracks, left and ahead. On a tree, slightly right, is a large yellow and black sign stating 'No Bridle-path — Strictly No Horses'. Indeed the track is not a bridleway but it is most certainly a public footpath. So go forward on the track ahead to join a right hand fence near the sign. Now follow the clear track along the edge of the woodland with the fence and pasture on your right. Beginning to rise gently, your track starts to swing right a little and then leaves the fence at its corner to continue forward and slightly up through the trees.

Take your time over this next section which is a good stretch of mature oak woodland, understandably popular with the forest's deer population.

Though there are several side paths and tracks there is no difficulty following your route which gradually rises and follows a generally southerly direction. In a while your track merges with one coming in from the right and continues forward to rise a little more steeply. Reaching the woodland edge if you look over your shoulder you will see another yellow and black sign this time stating 'Footpath Only — Horses Keep Out'! Here there is a junction of ways and you go straight ahead into the hedged and fenced track to then arrive at a gate and stile left of 'Rosebine'.

Over the stile continue forward now on a broad, unsurfaced lane to then arrive at a T-junction with another lane. Turn right to return back to Callow Hill Methodist church and the A456, where just a short way left is The Royal Forester public house.

3

Nice 'n Easy

Blakedown

Mount Segg may be a pretentious name for a tree clad hillock standing at a mere 318 feet; but it does give rise to an exceptionally pretty walk with, at one end, an inviting walled garden and, at the other, a patch of sandy heathland where you would least expect it. Indeed this is a walk to relish rather than rush!

DISTANCE: 5 miles
MAPS: Landranger (1:50,000) 139
Pathfinder (1:25,000) 953
PARKING: Good off road parking in Deansford Lane
PUBLIC TRANSPORT: Midland Red West Services 192/292/193.
Travelling *from* Birmingham alight at the third bus stop after The Old House at Home (Deansford Lane — signed 'Bluntington'). Go back a few yards and go right along the lane, past Bissell Wood.
START/FINISH: Deansford Lane (GR 873772)

STARTING in Deansford Lane, opposite Bissell Wood, walk towards Deansford Farm and just before the entrance take the gate on the right and follow the bridleway forward and left as it crosses a stream and descends to another. At the second stream follow the bank and cross with the bridge to the opposite side where a distinct footpath goes right to follow the other bank below Mount Segg. Initially there are two paths running in parallel and only a few yards from each other. It doesn't matter which you follow, however, as eventually they merge anyway. The next three quarters of a mile is a mixed woodland nature reserve and it was here that I saw only my second Green Woodpecker!

Arriving at a gate and stile, cross to the hairpin bend and take the lower arm to pass Dunclent House — dodging the rabbits on the way. As you follow the drive its tarmac abruptly ends near 'The Woodlands' and, unsurfaced, it continues to meet another drive on a bend. From here you continue forward in the same direction to meet the A448 at Stone.

Turn right along the main road and then immediately left into Stanklyn Lane to reach a sharp right bend with a finger post. Behind it is a public footpath sign pointing left up a tarmac drive to a gate. Stop

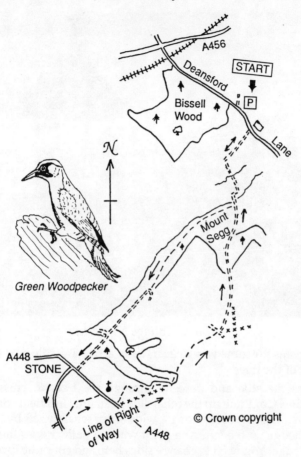

Green Woodpecker

© Crown copyright

at the gate and go over the stile on the right and follow the left hand hedge as far as a mature and nicely shaped oak tree. From here you will see the church spire and a little to the left of it — in front of a detached house — a stile. Cross it and head directly for the spire and the fence stile giving access to the A448.

Go right along the road until just beyond Butts Lane where on the left is a gate and a public footpath sign. The sign points diagonally across the field but a path has been trodden clockwise around the perimeter and this would seem to be the route preferred by the landowner. If you choose to follow the edge, and this is the route described here, you will have the advantage of seeing the walled garden and decorative buildings of Stone Cottage Nurseries. So, continue along the field edge

Stone Cottage Nurseries

as it zigzags for some way to eventually arrive at a stile next to a gate at the end of the trees.

Cross the stile and descend through the trees to cross a stream footbridge. Continue up the other side to emerge in a field corner where a left turn will take you along a wide strip, sensibly left by the farmer, with a hedge on the left. At a point where a path crosses there is a gap in the hedge. You need to change sides here and continue forward, now with the hedge on your right, to meet a cross track in the top corner of the field.

Turn right along the cross track for about 10 yards and then left into a field so that you follow the left boundary back on your original line. Follow this bridleway for two fields over what is a low rounded ridge with views left to the Clee Hills and right to the Clent Hills. In a corner by trees a hunter's gate awaits you. Go through it to join a soft sandy path onto an area of heathland. Continue with the path as it bends and descends into a shallow valley and widens into a track. This is a main track and you keep to it as it follows the bottom of Mount Segg, tending left, to arrive at the stream bridge that you crossed on your outward journey. Now simply retrace your steps back to the start of this relaxing walk.

4

To the Boiling Well

Little Stretton

Because of its striking beauty the area around Ashes Hollow is very popular, particularly in the summer months, so pick your time well to fully enjoy the day. Little Stretton has some interesting old buildings and is worthy of a closer examination. Whatever you do, don't forget your camera on this walk!

DISTANCE: 6 miles
MAPS: Landranger (1:50,000) 137
Pathfinder (1:25,000) 910
PARKING: Roadside in Little Stretton
PUBLIC TRANSPORT: (*Add 3 miles*) British Rail, Church Stretton. From the town centre walk south along the B4370 (a normally quiet and pleasant road) for about 1½ miles to Little Stretton.
START/FINISH: Little Stretton (GR 443919)

THERE is a pretty, black and white, thatched — but twentieth century — church in Little Stretton: on the other side of the road is the Ragleth Inn. On the same side as the Ragleth Inn, and opposite the church, are the 'Ancient House' cottages. Between the cottages and the inn is a tiny lane that goes west to shortly arrive at a T-junction and a stream. Having followed it to this point now go right to pass Brook House and soon meet a ford and footbridge. Cross the footbridge and go immediately right over a step stile into a camp site.

With the stream on your right walk through the site to cross another step stile into a long, narrow pasture. Passing through this you will come to a third step stile and a National Trust sign. Cross over and walk the short distance to a footbridge where you cross to the opposite bank of the stream to continue in the same direction as before. Immediately passing a cottage you enter Ashes Hollow.

You now follow Ashes Hollow for two miles and on the way you will meet several side valleys — some wet, some dry — but always you stay with the main valley and its stream. Occasionally the path will cross to the opposite side of the stream but each time it is only for a very short distance and the path always returns to the right hand bank, as shown

© Crown copyright

on the sketch map. As you continue forward with the valley it begins to narrow and the path is very close to the stream in places. In other places the path is rocky so naturally take extra care when conditions are wet underfoot. At any time of the year the colours on the surrounding hills are quite breathtaking. So, take a deep breath and prepare yourself for a walk through a picture postcard!

After following the stream for some way you will eventually arrive at a tributary stream issuing from a valley on the right. Your way forward is with the primary stream and valley, left. Here you have a choice, either to follow the path immediately next to the primary stream — which can involve a little minor scrambling — or to take a higher route. The higher path is easier and in any event soon rejoins the stream. This is the one now described, the lower one being self evident.

At the juncture of the streams go right with the tributary for 10 yards and then cross it. You are now below a rock outcrop and above you will see a slight gap with a well worn route through it and over the outcrop. On the outcrop continue upwards with the path and follow it as it contours the main valley side and then descends to rejoin the main stream side path. Continue walking upstream and then pass through a narrower part of the valley which, after a short distance, opens out so that your path becomes wider.

After a particularly pleasant stretch of stream-side walking the path starts to swing right as the hollow begins to narrow slightly again. Stay with the clear path as its angle of rise increases. The stream has of course diminished in size but it still soothes as it tumbles down the hollow.

Thatched church at Little Stretton

Reaching the head of the valley, your path now swings right towards Boiling Well which is not what its name might suggest. It is simply a small area of wet moorland and the watershed for Ashes Hollow. The path now skirts just above the wetland and soon joins the metalled Portway at a marker post.

On the Portway turn left for 35 yards and on the bend take the broad gravel track on the right to follow it the short distance to a low brow. Cresting the brow you will meet a broad cross track with vehicle barrier posts on the left. Turn left through the posts and walk the short distance up to the triangulation pillar and toposcope on Pole Bank.

At 1693 feet Pole Bank is the highest point on the Long Mynd and is also higher than any of the surrounding hills. To the west you can see

Corndon Hill and the Stiperstones whilst to the east is Caer Caradoc — reputedly the scene of Caractacus' last stand against the Romans — and also The Lawley and The Wrekin.

Leaving the summit walk the track south, heading for a square of trees surrounding Pole Cottage — now just a tin shed! Your track re-joins the Portway just before Pole Cottage and here you turn right along the tarmac to pass the square of trees. Beyond the trees continue with the Portway for 250 yards to arrive at a marker post on the left indicating the way to Little Stretton.

Turn left to join this broad, scenic track and follow it to a shallow dip with a fairly large area of sheep cropped grass. Here there is a junction where the track splits. Yours is the left hand one and as a means of identifying it look in the turf for a flat piece of concrete measuring approximately 3 ft. × 4 ft. This slab is very close to the demarcation point for your left track and you should readily see the line ahead as it passes through the fern and heather and then contours around the left flank of a hillside.

So, having identified your way now follow it as it contours around the hillside above Ashes Hollow. To your left you will be able to identify the route you took during the first half of the walk. The path now rounds the hillside and then descends towards a shallow saddle. Ahead and across the saddle you will see the line of your track heading up and forward and then around the right flank of the next hill.

Arriving at the saddle cross it and pass through the low earth embankment of Cross Dyke to then rise with the grassy track and follow it as it flanks right around this second hill. The valley now on your right is Callow Hollow and you stay with this track as it eventually swings left, away from Callow Hollow, and gradually descends to the saddle overlooking Small Batch. Beyond and right can be seen the Vale of Stretton with Little Stretton at the foot of Small Batch.

On the saddle immediately above the batch your track now swings right to gradually descend above Small Batch (left) and below a hilltop (right). Soon meeting a fence the track now descends quite steeply left with it to arrive at a gate at the bottom of the batch. Go through the gate and then forward to pass a house and the entrance to the camp site. Ahead is the ford and footbridge of journey's end.

5

The King's Manor

Kinver

At the turn of the century, Kinver Edge was known by the Midland masses as 'Little Switzerland'. Today's much travelled public might think this a rather fanciful description but nonetheless it does give an indication of the topography and indeed the importance of this green oasis. The highest part of the edge is a mere 538 feet but still gives tremendous views of the surrounding countryside and the distant Clent, Clee, Malvern and Cotswold Hills.

The Norman Conquest saw Kinver as a royal manor and also the centre of a royal forest — several medieval kings visited Kinver on hunting expeditions. In later centuries the village was an important market town and situated on a prime route between Chester and the South-West. Today its Norman church, together with the number of inns and the nature of the High Street, testifies to its past importance.

This walk takes in the greater part of Kinver Edge and then crosses the landscape previously seen from the escarpment; thus making a stimulating, circular route.

DISTANCE: 6 miles
MAPS: Landranger (1:50,000) 138
Pathfinder (1:25,000) 933
PARKING: Lay-by below Holy Austin Rock
PUBLIC TRANSPORT: (*Add 1 mile*) West Midlands service 242 (Cradley Heath/Stourbridge/Kinver). Alight in High Street, Kinver. Go west along High Street, then turn left at the Plough and Harrow along Stone Lane. After about half a mile, where a road on the right goes off to Bridgnorth, go through trees on the left into an open area and take the path by the National Trust sign.
START/FINISH: Holy Austin Rock (GR 836836)

L EAVING the lay-by at the bottom of Holy Austin Rock take the path running east parallel to the road to the National Trust sign and then the steps up to the first level of rock dwellings.

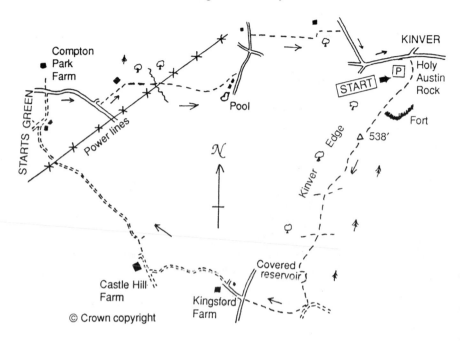

© Crown copyright

Holy Austin Rock — reputedly a hermit's home in the dim distant past — is a fascinating feature where for centuries families have lived in the substantial rock houses, the last only being re-housed around 1950! A hill fort, dating from the time of the Mercian King Wulfere, stands near the highest point. Today the rock dwellings and Edge are in the care of the National Trust whilst 'next-door' — and in the next county — is Kingsford Country Park.

Bearing left, follow the path around the base of the rock and then up more steps to the higher level. Here traces of the space and comfort enjoyed by generations of 'cave dwellers' can clearly be seen. Sadly parts have been vandalised in recent years so that certain sections have needed to be closed off, while some have even been restored.

Having explored this unusual housing estate continue forward, go down a few steps, then swing right back to the open sandy and grassy area where, going left and after a short but strenuous climb, you will emerge on the ridge top near a fine toposcope which will enable you to pick out many features in the surrounding countryside. Go right along the escarpment edge with the Staffordshire Way signs, to pass the hill fort embankments and a trig point. After a spell of stimulating ridge walking

16

you will arrive at a meeting of three long distance footpaths; the Staffordshire Way (92 miles), the North Worcestershire Path (21 miles) and the Worcestershire Way (36 miles).

Rock Houses at Kinver

Continuing in the same direction, but now following the Worcestershire Way, bear left by a wooden hide and follow a high fence around a covered reservoir to arrive at a second wooden barrier. Here there are two paths going right, the furthest one is a bridleway with a blue marker and the nearest is the Worcestershire Way with a yellow one. Follow the yellow sign to another wooden barrier, then follow another sign right as it leads down a grassy path and through a tranquil hollow to a junction with a broad track. Here the Worcestershire Way goes left and here is where you leave it. Instead go through the barrier to follow the narrow footpath opposite and soon emerge at a lane and footpath sign.

Cross the lane at the T-junction and follow the narrower one opposite as it rises to pass Kingsford Farm and become an unsurfaced lane. Now follow it all the way until it joins another track at Castle Hill Cottage. Go right along this to Castle Hill Farm and where it bears left you go straight ahead over a stile, next to a hunter's gate, and across a sloping pasture to exit at another gate and stile. You now have a superb view of Kinver Edge on your right. Continue forward along a broader track and in a very short while swing right with it as it follows a right hand hedge. Follow this way for almost a mile along a minor ridge until it meets a cross track at Starts Green. Turn right and follow this new track to a road, ignoring a footpath sign on the left.

The junction of three long distance paths

At the road turn right and follow it for approximately 400 yards where you meet a broad track coming in from the left. Just a few yards beyond this is a waymarked stile which you cross to enter a field. Follow the left boundary to a second field and cross this heading towards the hedge opposite and just left of the overhead lines. Here you will see two marker posts which — although they can be overgrown in summer — indicate a gap in the hedge and the way down through trees and over a stream. On the other side of the stream ignore the stile on the left and continue up the embankment into a field. Go diagonally right across this very large field aiming for the far right corner where there is another stile.

Cross the stile and follow the green elevated path — to your right and below is a pool. Clay pigeon shooting takes place here at times, but don't worry! Marshalls ensure that shooting stops whenever walkers appear on the path. Arriving at a gate into 'The Lydiates' go into the farm and, keeping to the left of the farm buildings, follow the way-marks into a drive to pass houses and arrive at a tarmac lane.

Turn left along the lane and follow it to crossroads where you go directly across and along the lane signed for 'Compton ¾, Enville 3¼'. After about 100 yds, just before 'Bannut Tree', a gateway on the right leads into a field. Go through it and directly across this large field – left of the fence – to the woodland edge opposite aiming to the right of some farm buildings. Arriving at the trees go left and then right at the corner to join a farm track leading to a lane. Here go right to a crossroads and then left back to your starting point.

6

Deer Spotting

Cannock Chase

As befits a former Royal Forest, Cannock Chase sustains a substantial deer population and Brocton Field is one of the best places to spot them — but be early! Indeed the whole of this walk is excellent for all forms of wildlife — foxes, badgers and water fowl abound whilst the surrounding heath, wetland and forest provide a varied habitat for a wide range of bird species.

DISTANCE: 6 miles
MAPS: Landranger (1:50,000) 127
Pathfinder (1:25,000) 850 & 871
PARKING: Chase Road Corner car park, Brocton Field
PUBLIC TRANSPORT: (*Add about 4½ miles.*) West Midlands Service 951 (Birmingham - Hednesford). Alight at Pye Green Corner. Go back a few yards and cross Pye Green Road into the continuation of Broadhurst Green, heading towards the Telecom tower and passing this on your right. After about a mile pass the German War Cemetery on the right and then, after about another three quarters of a mile, pass the entrance, also on the right, to Anson's Bank car park followed shortly by another entrance to the same car park. A little further on turn right along the road into Chase Road Corner car park (about 400 yds.).
START/FINISH: Chase Road Corner car park (GR 980176)

IN Chase Road Corner car park there is a public footpath sign next to a vehicle barrier pole. Carrying the symbol of the Heart of England Way — a long distance regional footpath stretching eighty miles from Cannock Chase to Chipping Camden in the Cotswolds — this sign also points the way to the start of your walk. So, following the sign through the barrier, walk up the gravel track in a north-easterly direction to the bank above Womere.

Womere is the Old English name for an upland bog, though hereabouts the paths are well drained. During the Great War of 1914-1918 much of the surrounding area was a huge military camp and today occasional traces of the buildings can still be found amongst the turf and heather.

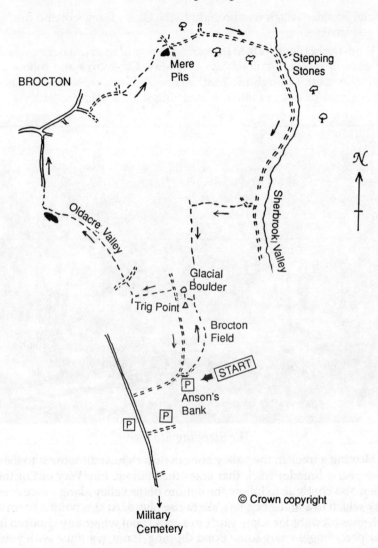

BROCTON

Mere Pits

Stepping Stones

Oldacre Valley

Sherbrook Valley

N

Glacial Boulder

Trig Point

Brocton Field

START

P

Anson's Bank

P

P

© Crown copyright

Military Cemetery

On the bank, and at a junction, is another footpath sign where you turn left to follow a broad level track. At a right hand junction you will meet another footpath sign where you continue forward to ignore the right turn. This line will bring you to another, wider, junction where to the left you will see a Staffordshire Way sign and at 637 feet, a triangulation pillar. Go to the pillar and from there the few yards to the erratic

21

Glacial Boulder which was brought to the Chase from Scotland during the last Ice Age.

From the boulder walk to the surfaced strip of road just below where opposite is another Staffordshire Way sign. Cross over and follow its distinctive path through the heathland and over a cross track to then begin a gradual descent into the beautiful, shallow Oldacre Valley.

The Stepping Stones

Meeting a track in the valley bottom turn right and follow it to then cross over a broader track that takes the Staffordshire Way out of the valley. You continue to follow the bottom of the valley along a nice easy track which in a while begins a slight rise ahead. At this point a narrow path goes off right for a few yards to a small pool where any children in your party might enjoy some pond dipping. If not, continue with your track as it begins its gentle rise and then splits left and right. The left fork continues to rise but you take the right hand one to contour slightly above the valley bottom — ignoring side tracks — to then enter trees at a right hand chestnut paling fence. Continue through the trees to be joined by another paling fence coming in from the left. Here there is a footbridge which you cross to the fence corner to then continue along a clear path, with the fence on your left, to quickly arrive at a large pool with many water-fowl. The pool is a former quarry dramatically restored by nature with a helping hand from man.

Follow the fence along the sandstone edge of the pool to then follow the track as it starts to swing right, beyond a 'Danger, No Swimming Here' sign. Passing through trees for a short way the track emerges onto a flat grassy area and continues through the middle to reach metal gates with a wooden kissing gate. Go through to reach the tarmac of Oldacre Lane.

Mere Pits

Now follow the lane for some distance until after passing Brocton Village Hall you arrive at a junction in front of Pinfold Cottage. Go left and then immediately right along the side of the 'village green' to the T-junction with Pool Lane, Brocton. Go right along Pool Lane to pass Heather Hill on the right and then arrive at Brook Lane. Turn right up Brook Lane which immediately before a junction becomes unsurfaced. Turn left at the junction and follow the unmade road to a point beyond the houses where, now more as a track, it bends sharp left while on the right of the bend is a vehicle barrier.

Go through the vehicle barrier where your new track immediately splits left and right. You take the left fork to follow the base of a hillock and so walk through the pleasant Mere Valley. Continue on the gravelly track as it progresses through heath and heather to eventually bring you to a pool amongst the trees on the right. Pass the pool — Mere Pits — to a junction of many tracks where there is a marker post. Here you need to continue directly ahead along the unsurfaced road signed for 'Punchbowl ½ m'. Follow this road for a while until arriving at a T-junction with a similar road and with another marker post. Turn right here to follow the direction for 'Stepping Stones ¾ m' — you are now entering the Sherbrook Valley.

At the end of the three quarters of a mile you will reach a crossing track with the Stepping Stones, a very popular local beauty spot, on your left. You however stay on your original route to keep the Sherbrook on your left and to follow the Staffordshire Way sign forward along the valley.

About half a mile past the Stepping Stones your way leaves the trees to pass through open heathland. A shorter distance on — and just before a picnic area on the left — you will arrive at a Staffordshire Way sign pointing right and up a side valley.

Go right with this signpost on a broad track to soon leave it as it swings right into another valley. Instead, at the bend, you continue straight ahead to follow the Staffordshire Knot marker up the left hand of the two side valleys. Stay with the clear track as it ascends to the bank top and a T-junction with a cross track. Here another Staffordshire Way sign takes you left along the track and back to the triangulation pillar. Again join the Glacial Boulder and descend to the road but this time turn left to follow the tarmac back to Chase Road Corner car park.

7

Iron Age Early Warning

Cannock Chase

At Moors Gorse pumping station there is a very convenient car park and picnic area which provides the launch of a circular walk across part of Cannock Chase. This part of the Chase is quite heavily afforested and as a result it is always subject to forestry operations. It should be remembered that the consequence of these operations is the frequent appearance and disappearance of forest roads and tracks. Subsidence is also a fairly common feature of Cannock Chase whose underground coal seams have been exploited for centuries. Nonetheless the Chase fully justifies its status as an Area of Outstanding Natural Beauty (AONB).

Apart from the natural beauty of Cannock Chase this walk also takes in an Iron Age hill fort and a nature reserve.

DISTANCE: 6½ miles
MAPS: Landranger (1:50,000) 128
Pathfinder (1:25,000) 872
PARKING: Car parking and picnic area at Moors Gorse. Car park at Castle Ring
PUBLIC TRANSPORT: (*Add 3 miles*) British Rail, Hednesford. See box on p. 27
START/FINISH: Moors Gorse picnic area (GR 024151)

NEAR the pumping station and car park there is a bridleway and Heart of England Way (HEW) sign which points up a valley. At times the scene of dog sled racing — with wheels of course! — this forestry road is also the start of your walk. So, following the direction of the sign and ignoring two tracks on the right and two pools on the left reach an incline on a left bend. On your right you will see a pool which is the oddly named Seven Springs.

Some forty years ago this little hollow was dry except for a tiny stream fed by two, not seven, springs, one emerging from under a rock and the other bubbling out of the sandy soil. Since then subsidence due

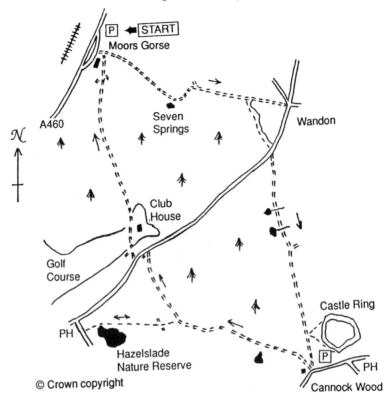

to mining activity has caused the hollow to flood and today only the spring at the rock is still visible.

From the pool continue with the bend and follow it round to a marker post. Ignoring the signed path for Miflins Valley on the left, stay with your forestry road and follow it towards Wandon. Shortly passing two forestry houses you will then pass on the right a turning area and then on the same side two adjacent vehicle barriers. Go right through the second barrier to follow a broad path behind the attractive Camping and Caravanning Club site at Wandon. Older maps show a Youth Hostel here but it was in fact burnt down very many years ago.

Beyond the camp site the path meets an unclassified road which can be rather busy. Cross over to the gas pipeline post opposite where a broad track — with a HEW sign — goes forward and down to follow power line poles. Ignoring cross and side tracks descend to pass over two pool outlets at the valley bottom. Ignoring a track on the left

26

continue with another HEW sign forward and up the other side of the valley still following the line of poles. Go over a cross track at another HEW sign and continue up to reach the highest point of the track which is in fact just before the second of two wooden pylons with double poles. As a positive means of identification the second pylon has a yellow circular disc, containing a black letter 'C', attached to it. Here turn left and then take the third path on the right to gain the embankments of Castle Ring.

This Iron Age hill fort was built around 500BC and is a well preserved example covering nine acres and comprising several ramparts and ditches. Originally protected by a timber stockade on its main rampart, and by massive wooden gates at its entrance, it would have given scattered farming communities a safe refuge in times of trouble. It may have been occupied as late as AD500. The site includes the remains of a much later building, thought to be a medieval hunting lodge associated with the royal forest of Cannock Chase.

At 794 feet, Castle Ring is the highest point on the Chase and it would have provided an excellent 'Early Warning System' to defenders. Certainly today it affords wide views across the remainder of the Chase and the Trent Valley.

Public Transport

From Hednesford station go up the steps and turn right along Market Street. At the traffic lights turn left along Rugeley Road and, just past the car park on the left, cross the road and take the bridle-path which goes beside the entrance to Hednesford War Memorial onto Hednesford Hill Common.

Go straight forward over the common until the path drops down to some buildings and a rough road. Turn right along the road and pass through a gate. After about 100 yds turn left beside a fenced area and climb up the path, after a few yards passing a post marked 'Waymarked Walk' and 'Car Park'. Follow the Car Park direction: over to the right you will see a newly constructed concrete reservoir.

Ignoring any side and cross tracks go forward maintaining a generally east-north-east direction until you drop down to a house and the road at a T-junction. Cross the road and follow the turning signed 'Beaudesert Golf Course' to reach The Hazleslade public house. Turn right along Cannock Wood Street to reach the entrance to Hazleslade Nature Reserve on the left. Go into the nature reserve to pick up the walk at the point in the text marked ▦➤ on p 28.

Leaving the fort retrace your steps to the track you left earlier to then continue beyond your second marker pylon and in your original direction head towards a vehicle barrier, buildings and a house. Immediately before the house go right along a broad track at the edge of the forest and follow it as it angles back a little deeper into the trees. In a while the track brings you to a pool on your left at a junction with another track. Behind the pool nature is making a determined and successful effort to colonise colliery spoil heaps.

Leaving the pool continue forward along your original track and in a while you will see on the left, and through the trees, the long compound of a saw mill and 'Mals Building Supplies'. Adjacent to the end of the compound a track appears to go left but it is a dead end — ignore it. Instead stay with your original track for almost another 50 yards to a point where your track starts to bear right. Here go left through the trees on a broad and well defined path which brings you to the fence around Hazelslade Nature Reserve. Go through the fence gap to turn right for a few feet and then left along a smaller path to reach a gate and stile. Beyond the gate follow a good, grassy path to the Reserve's pool.

➠ Having explored the Reserve make your way back to your previous forest track where you now turn left to continue the original direction. Initially following more wooden poles, in a while you will reach the road opposite the entrance to Beaudesert Golf Club. A left turn along the road takes you past two houses and, in a further 150 yards, to a track on the right with a rotten vehicle barrier. Follow this track as it doubles back, almost parallel to the road, and then goes left to join another track at a T-junction. Here go right where in a few yards you will see a marker post on the right stating 'Moors Gorse 1m'. Quickly swinging left your new track passes through the open ground to the left of the Club House.

Soon entering trees again follow the clear track forward — ignoring right and left turns — to descend into a valley and arrive at the rear of the pumping station. Here there is a junction of paths and tracks where you now bear right and then left to arrive back at Moors Gorse car park and picnic area.

8

A Battle Royal

Salt Village

Salt village is an attractive mix of ancient and modern tucked away from the busy A51, the railway, the canal, and the river Trent; all of which funnel through the narrow Trent Valley. Boasting a twelfth century thatched pub, the village doesn't owe its name to that well known mineral but more likely to the Old English word Sallow, which is just another name for a willow. As willows enjoy wetlands, and seeing the close proximity of the river, its not too difficult to accept this interpretation.

DISTANCE: 6½ miles
MAPS: Landranger (1:50,000) 127
Pathfinder (1:25,000) 850
PARKING: Limited roadside at Salt; Good lay-by on B5066
BUS SERVICE: Service 492 (Bassett's) Stafford to Eccleshall (no Sunday service). Alight at Salt
START/FINISH: Salt Village (GR 958278)

OUR walk starts just beyond The Holly Bush Inn at a public footpath sign opposite the telephone kiosk. Following the direction of the sign, pass between the houses and then cross a stile at the side of the gate ahead to enter a field. Now follow the left hand hedge for about 85 yds to its protruding corner, then go half left across a slope and aim for the top far left corner of a large stand of trees. Just before the top of the bank there is a fenced off area where you need to pass between it and the woodland edge to gain the top corner.

At the corner of the woodland bear right along the edge of the field, with the trees on your right, to a gate. Go through the gate and, ignoring one on the right, immediately cross a track to pass through the gate opposite. Through the gate you will see a stile in line with a tree house. Cross it and walk with the hedge on your left to pass left of the tree house, a dovecot and Leatop Farm where you will arrive at another stile at the side of a gate.

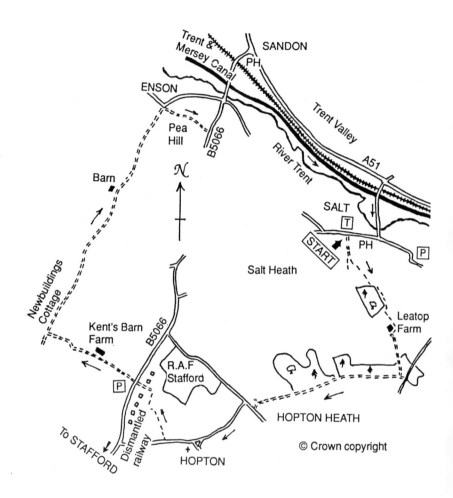

© Crown copyright

In the next field descend half right to pass just left of wooden stables where there is a stile onto the farm drive. Turn left along the drive and pass houses to arrive at a T-junction of tracks on the hilltop. Following the bridleway right, which gives brief views across the valley before trees obscure the scene, continue on this line for three quarters of a mile ignoring any turns on the way. About half-way along this three quarter mile stretch the main track swings right. You, however, continue forward on the now grassy bridleway where, just before its end it swings left to meet a road.

*The Holly Bush – reputedly the second
oldest inn in England*

As you follow this bridleway, on your left is Hopton Heath which in 1643 was the site of a battle between Roundheads and Cavaliers where the protagonists fought all day to a standstill and a draw. Although an inconclusive result it demonstrated the importance of nearby Stafford which was held at the time by the Royalists. Outnumbered three to two the Royalists did have the advantage of 'Roaring Meg', an infamous cannon, which appears to have evened the odds. Casualties were remarkably light — less than 200 — and the Cavaliers were able to return to Stafford. Two months later they lost it for good!

At the road turn right and then immediately left to follow a lane into the attractive village of Hopton. In the village pass two junctions left and then a brick bus shelter right — note its 'Best Kept Village' plaque — after which the lane descends to a left bend where, on the right, is 'Bank Top' house. There is a footpath post hidden in the garden's holly hedge! Here turn right onto the broad track that passes right of the house to reach a white metal gate into a field.

In the field follow the track with a hedge on your left and an embankment on your right to soon reach a gate in a left hand fence. Go through and follow the direction of the way-mark arrow down the field,

31

with the left hedge, to the bottom corner. In the corner turn right and still following the hedge arrive at a green roofed barn. On your left is a bridge over the dismantled railway and which takes you to the B5066.

Cross the road to enter the farm road directly opposite and follow it to pass Kent's Barn Farm and other dwellings. Beyond the houses the way becomes a clear track which then swings right to enter a field and fade. In the field your way is to follow the left hand hedge towards the solitary Newbuildings Cottage and in the field corner go through a collapsed and overgrown gate which is negotiable.

Immediately to your right is a stile in a fence and this is now your direction for almost a mile. Following this north-north-easterly direction you cross a total of six stiles — in varying conditions — and six fields. For the first two fields you follow the right hand hedge, the third you cross the centre, the fourth and fifth you follow the left hedge but in the fifth you cross a stile near a large oak tree and before the end of the field. In the sixth field your way forward is through a wide avenue of trees to reach a stone barn.

This barn will be of interest to those with a penchant for old buildings. Possibly spanning several centuries the base is made of large rectangular stone blocks while other parts consist of oak timbers and differing types of brickwork. The roof is modern corrugated asbestos sheeting!

Keeping to the right of the barn your path now becomes a substantial hedged track which in half a mile brings you, via a gate at each end, to the corner of a lane at Enson. At the corner a hedged, sunken and well trodden bridleway goes sharp and immediately right to climb up Pea Hill. It then joins the B5066 where a left turn will, in just under a quarter of a mile, take you across the adolescent River Trent to Sandon Lock on the Trent and Mersey Canal.

Finding the way onto the towpath can be interesting. The access is so close to, and below, the road that it is not immediately noticeable — but it is there. Joining the towpath follow it right (south-east) for a mile. Look out for an original 1819 mile-post shortly after joining the canal.

Reaching bridge number 82 go under it to join the road. Turn left along the road and then cross the River Trent to enter Salt village.

9

Walk a Straight Line

Wenlock Edge

In days gone by, a single track railway ran along the slopes of Wenlock Edge. Running from Craven Arms to Ironbridge it was closed in 1962 and has long since been dismantled: it is now in the care of the National Trust. As such it contributes some three woodland miles to this scenic walk.

The combination of woodland and limestone escarpment also provides ideal habitat for several species of wild orchid. Indeed, the very rare bee orchid has been spotted in this area and other varieties, such as the pyramidal orchid, are fairly common.

> DISTANCE: 7½ miles
> MAPS: Landranger (1:50,000) 137
> Pathfinder (1:25,000) 910
> PARKING: Wenlock Edge Car Park (Care: There are two Wenlock Edge car parks. One is just outside Much Wenlock; yours is near Presthope, grid reference 583976)
> START/FINISH: Wenlock Edge Car Park (GR 583976)

STARTING from the Wenlock Edge car park near Presthope, go through the wooden gate near the entrance that bears the Shropshire Way 'soaring buzzard' symbol. In a few yards, on a bend, is a direction post with red and green arrows. Go left with the green arrow indicating Easthope Wood and take the steps down to join and follow a sunken path as it descends the Edge. In a short distance another marker post with a green arrow takes you left out of the sunken path to then swing right along a made path through the woodland. Gradually descending, this path brings you to the tarmac of the Hughley road where you turn right for a few yards until opposite a farm road you will see another green marker on the left.

Following the marker into the trees the path immediately splits left and right. Though the left hand one is the correct route it can be very muddy and the right hand one is simply a trodden diversion — which can, however, also be muddy! Whichever you follow you ascend the

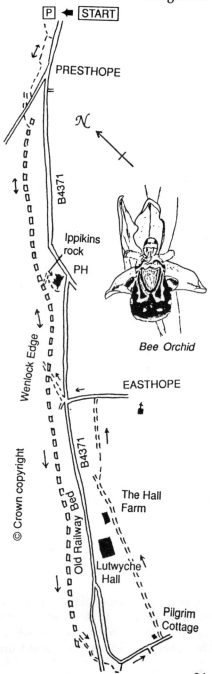

PRESTHOPE

𝒩

B4371

Ippikins
rock

PH

Bee Orchid

Wenlock Edge

EASTHOPE

© Crown copyright

B4371

Old Railway Bed

The Hall
Farm

Lutwyche
Hall

Pilgrim
Cottage

quite steep bank where they merge just before reaching the hunter's gate and stile onto the dismantled railway track. Joining the track, opposite you will see a post marking the path that rises to Ippikins Rock. This is not the one you want, instead you turn right to follow the old railway line as it keeps a level course along the flank of Wenlock Edge.

Continue following the old line as it progresses through woodland, with occasional glimpses of the Shropshire countryside through the trees on the right, until arriving at a track on the left with a marker post and green arrow indicating the way to Ippikins Rock. The rock in fact provides a tremendous viewing platform and as a result is well worth the detour. There is also a pub, The Wenlock Edge Inn, nearby. Turn left up the slope where in a short while you arrive at another marker post which directs you right to a step onto a path. Now follow this path as it rises to pass right of a rock face to then ascend to a stile over which is the rock and your view point.

Returning from Ippikins Rock just retrace your steps back to the railway bed where of course you now turn left to continue your journey. In a while you will cross a railway bridge over a lane and then

34

immediately pass through a gate. Note this spot for your return journey!

Immediately ahead is a second gate which continues your walk along the railway through Northway Wood, crossing *en route* a second railway bridge and then a third, but smaller, one which you can easily miss. Continue until arriving at a point where ahead the track looks like a regular avenue of trees. Immediately before this point is a sign pointing left and declaring

⇐ PATH — NO ACCESS BEYOND THIS POINT

Go left with the arrow along the obvious track and then immediately right as it gradually ascends the Edge to a gate onto the B4371.

Cross the road where opposite is a National Trust sign together with a bridleway sign and a gate. Beyond the gate follow the bridleway uphill and shortly go right with it to a marker post at a T-junction with a broader track. Here go left with the direction of the blue arrow and in a short way meet another T-junction of tracks where you go left a short distance to join the narrow tarmac lane on a bend at the top of the Edge.

Turning right, follow the lane around the bend and continue with it to a point where the tarmac goes right and the way ahead is a wide track. Walk forward on the track to a house — Pilgrim Cottage — immediately beyond which is a gate on the left with a Shropshire Way symbol. Turn left here and pass along the side of Pilgrim Cottage now on a clear broad track at the top edge of the field. Arriving at a gate across the track go over the fence stile at the side and continue forward with a fence on your right. You soon arrive at the corner of a brick wall that surrounds the impressive Lutwyche Hall and its gardens.

Still continuing forward, with the wall on your left and the fence on your right, head for the gate in the fence immediately before a black barn at The Hall Farm. Passing through the gate and standing immediately before the end of the barn you will see to your right a gate leading into a field. This carries a yellow way-mark arrow and a Shropshire Way sign.

Pass through this waymarked gate and go immediately left with the fence, along and behind the barn, where in a short distance the fence will bring you to a corner and a hunter's gate next to a water trough. Go through the gate and turn instantly right to follow a farm track and the right hand fence to another waymarked gate. Through the gate follow the grassy track forward and, passing trees on your right, aim for the cottage ahead. Just before the cottage is a waymarked gate, go through it and forward to follow the garden hedge into a hedged track. Follow the track to soon arrive at a tarmacked lane. If you wish to visit Easthope and its attractive little church then turn right along the lane — if not, turn left and follow the lane uphill to the B4371.

At the crossroads go directly across into the minor road opposite and then turn immediately right along the narrow surfaced lane signed for Easthope Wood. Pass the partly hidden 'No Through Road' sign and descend with the lane until reaching the railway bridge you crossed and noted earlier.

Rejoining the old railway bed go right and across the bridge to follow the track all the way back to the hunter's gate and stile that you passed over not long after the start of your walk. Go left over the stile and follow the muddy path back down to the Hughley road where you turn right and then, after a few yards, left to join the waymarked path that retraces your steps back to the car park.

10

A 'Nimrod' Theme

Onibury

*Many will know Elgar's Enigma Variations and in particular the score that
starts very quietly, builds to a crescendo and then slowly fades to the end. The
piece is Nimrod and, although he was a native of Worcestershire rather than
Shropshire, Elgar perfectly captures the mood of this walk and the countryside
it moves through. A gentle beginning rises to a dramatic landscape and then
gradually descends back to the Onny Valley. Instant mood music!*

DISTANCE: 7¾ miles
MAPS: Landranger (1:50,000) 137
Pathfinder (1:25,000) 931 & 951
PARKING: Roadside at Onibury and Whittytree; Car park at Stokesay
Castle
PUBLIC TRANSPORT: Midland Red West. Service 192/292 (Birmingham
- Ludlow); then Service 435 (Ludlow - Church Stretton). Alight at Onibury.
START/FINISH: Onibury (GR 455792)

STARTING from the small village of Onibury, follow the A49(T) across
the level crossing and the River Onny to then turn right for a few
yards along a minor road signed for Aldon and Clungunford. At
the next junction go right along the lane signed for Aldon and just
beyond the left bend go right with the signed public footpath through
the farmyard of Stepaside Farm. Keeping to the right of the barns and
farm buildings go forward to pass through a farmyard gate — it can be
muddy at times — and then walk on to meet two gates in front of you.
Take the right hand one to follow a grassy terraced track, with a hedge
on your left, to another gate into a field. In the field continue forward to
cross a stile next to the railway line which you follow to cross two more
fields and two more stiles. The third stile takes you through a few
isolated trees to the pointed fence corner around a substantial woodland.

Ordnance Survey maps show the path now entering this woodland,
following the lower edge and then exiting from the trees back towards
the railway line. However, at the time of writing the woodland is
impassable and the following short diversion — which judging from an

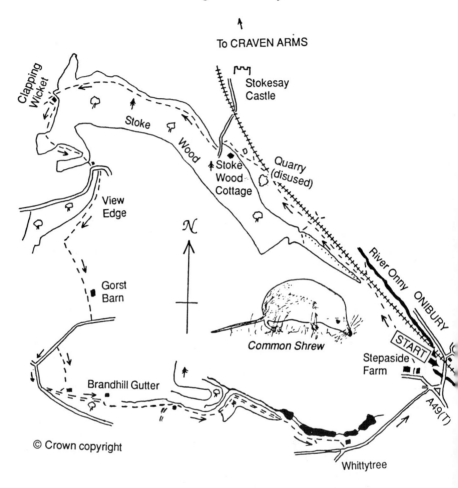

To CRAVEN ARMS

Clapping Wicket

Stokesay Castle

Stoke Wood

View Edge

Stoke Wood Cottage

Quarry (disused)

N

River Onny ONIBURY

Gorst Barn

Common Shrew

START

Stepaside Farm

A49(T)

Brandhill Gutter

© Crown copyright

Whittytree

'official' looking stile appears to be an 'official' diversion anyway — is recommended (see also the sketch map).

At the start of this substantial woodland continue forward to walk between the trees and the railway line. In a few yards you will see a metal kissing gate on the right which takes a footpath across the railway. Ignore this and continue forward a short distance to the official looking stile next to a gate. Cross over and follow a line between the trees and the railway where at the end of this field you will see a bridge under the railway to your right. Left and slightly ahead is a fence and stile which brings the Shropshire Way path — and the impenetrable one — out of the woods to join you. Go forward through the next field to cross a waymarked stile in the fence a little above the railway. On the other side go forward to pass right of the disused quarry and the old lime kilns. Now on a distinct track follow it until, near a solitary tree, it starts to drop to meet the railway again. Here you go half left and climb the bank to the hedge and fence at Stoke Wood Cottage. Go forward with the fence to the field corner where you will see a stile. Cross the stile and go up with the waymarked and hedged track to another way-mark post where you turn right to go through a gate and enter Stoke Wood. Now simply follow the woodland path, with occasional views across the Onny Valley to Stokesay Castle and Norton Camp. On the musical theme note the sudden change of mood when the deciduous woodland gives way to conifers.

After about a mile emerge from the trees at Clapping Wicket. Despite its imaginative name, this is merely an attractively restored cottage at the woodland edge. Ignoring the stile into a field on your right cross the stile in front, on the right side of the cottage, to then turn left to pass the front of it and so up to a marker pole on the woodland edge. Do not go over the stile behind but go right with the direction of the arrow and follow the edge of the trees to meet a clear track which enters the woodland. After a short way the track enters a sloping pasture and all you now have to do is follow the way-marks to the top of the hill and a narrow tarmac lane. Go left and then very shortly right over a stile to follow the edge woodland to a stile.

You have been gradually gaining altitude for the last two miles and are now on View Edge — well worth the effort for a well named place! On a clear day this is the perfect spot for a break while you take in the views.

Resuming the walk, your way forward is clear over another stile and almost in the corner of the next field you go left through a gap in the hedge and follow the direction post across the field to a gate. Through the gate follow the distinct track forward to pass the house at Gorst Barn and join the road. Turn right along the road until meeting the second field gate on your left, opposite some corrugated iron buildings.

Here a public footpath goes left through the gate and down the sloping field to follow the left hand hedge. Passing through two further gates it enters a narrow field and then goes a little right to follow a fence down to a stile at the side of a cottage and onto the track at the valley bottom. Here you would turn left but at the time of writing the footpath was not signed from the road and the second and third gates were in a collapsing state. However the County Council are aware of this and have scheduled it for attention so, hopefully, when you walk it, all will be clear.

Should this not be the case though, then simply continue along the road past the corrugated iron buildings until reaching a T-junction. Here go left and soon arrive at farm buildings and a red letter box on the right. Continue along the road for a further 20 yards beyond the letter box and on the left you will see a public bridleway sign pointing down a track. This is the start of the unusually named — but outstanding — Brandhill Gutter.

Follow the sign down the track and soon pass the stile mentioned above which is on your left just before the cottage. Walk past the cottage on the track to then pass through a gateway — passing two stiles on the right — to now reach, on the left, a white cottage and a wooden barn. Ahead of you is a wooden gate into a field while to your right is a metal gate. Pass through the right hand metal gate and swing left to follow the same line below the trees right and above the Gutter left. From here the way always keeps the Gutter on your left. Continue down the valley — ignore the wooden hunter's gate to the left on the opposite side of the Gutter — and at the end of the field go through a metal hunter's gate in the bottom corner.

This next section, about 300 yards, is an area of high bird cover through which Shropshire County Council have cleared the bridleway — work continues. With regular attention and usage this should remain clear but a stick can always be a useful tool! Continue forward through this section until meeting a drive coming down the hillside to a restored house. This is named 'Vale View' on the Definitive Map.

Join the drive and walk forward to pass immediately left of the house between it and the Gutter bottom. Immediately at the rear of the house you will see a long, steep flight of steps going right and up the embankment. This is the public footpath up to 'Green Lane', the tarmacked road. You ignore this however to continue straight ahead for 20 yards to a manhole cover and concrete blocks (possibly a cesspit) where you bear slightly left and down to pass between the Gutter bottom and a small pool.

Now continuing along the edge of the Gutter, which is often dry, follow it for a short distance to meet a hedged track coming in from the right. Carry on forward to pass a white cottage just discernible through the trees on the right to soon arrive at a waymarked step stile. Cross over and following the same line shortly meet another step stile in a fence corner. Cross this one also and still following the same line, and with the fence on your left, arrive at a cross fence.

At the time of writing there was a hurdle gate in this fence though this may well have been replaced with a stile in view of the County Council's continuing works.

Either way go through or over and walk just above the bottom of the sloping pasture heading towards trees. This pasture is part of the Rare Poultry Collection Farm and you may well see some different looking sheep! Passing a metal water trough reach a step stile in the bottom corner of the pasture and at the edge of the trees.

Cross the stile and initially follow a path along the left hand fence. It soon develops into a broad track near the junction of Brandhill Gutter and Aldon Gutter where it bears right to become a beautiful mixed woodland walk with lots of rhododendrons. Follow the track to pass the first of a series of pools and then go through a wooden gate into pasture.

Through the gate follow the grassy track along the valley bottom — ignoring a stile away on the right and at the top of the valley side — and continue towards farm buildings ahead. Soon the track rises gently towards them and then meets a stone wall to swing sharp right to a gate and so on to the road at the telephone kiosk and Whittytree.

Now turn left along the road for the quiet, gentle walk back to the Onny Valley and Onibury where excellent teas are served at the former Onibury railway station.

11

A Forest Not Too Far

Wyre Forest

This is a walk along the lesser known paths of the beautiful Wyre Forest. In parts, pleasing ridge walks give impressive views across the surrounding landscape.

DISTANCE: 8 miles
MAPS: Landranger (1:50,000) 138
Pathfinder (1:25,000) 952
PUBLIC TRANSPORT. Midland Red West service 192/292 — Birmingham/Kidderminster/Hereford. Alight at the Plough Inn, Far Forest.
PARKING: Various roadside points
START/FINISH: Plough Inn, Far Forest (GR 730744)

FROM the Plough Inn on the A4117 at Far Forest take the lane opposite and follow it until reaching a small white cottage — with a horse shoe — on the left, just after a bungalow named 'Cleestones'. Cross over the stile at the side to take the enclosed path along the edge of the cottage and its garden. Crossing another stile follow the field edge to emerge at the corner of a rough surfaced lane. Continue forward along Sugars Lane for about half a mile and turn left at a junction to pass a large private road sign. In a while, and opposite a yellow hydrant sign, a footpath goes left to descend to a footbridge over a stream. Cross the bridge and continue forward along a now hedged and fenced track, following it through a sharp right bend, and up to pass to the left of 'The Newells' cottage onto a narrow lane.

Here a right turn will take you on a short, pleasant diversion (about 250 yds.) to Dowles Brook after which retrace your steps to 'The Newells'.

Back at 'The Newells', continue to follow the narrow lane uphill and round a bend to a T-junction. Here go right along the road for about a third of a mile, on the way going right under the old railway bridge, and then left to a dip in the road where on the right you pass stone pillared ornamental gates with a sign 'Stepping Stones' — presumably the name of the house. Continue past these gates and — ignoring a bridleway sign pointing left — soon reach a metal kissing gate on the right. Go through the kissing gate and then quickly over three stiles onto a narrow lane.

Go right along the lane and follow it as it descends to cross the bridge over Lem Brook. Immediately pass the ornamental metal gates of 'Furnace Mill' on the left and rise with the lane as it now passes a finger

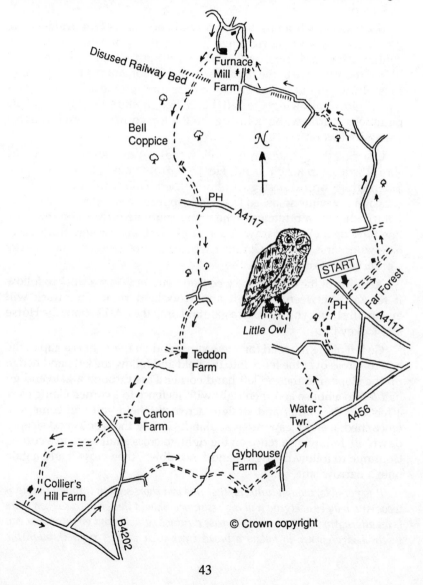

© Crown copyright

43

post and T-junction to descend and quickly arrive at a farm road on the left.

The line of this farm road, which has a sign 'Furnace Mill Stud' at the entrance, is a public right of way that does not appear on Ordnance Survey maps. However it does appear on the Definitive Map (path number 7R) and will at some time in the future be included on revised O.S. maps.

So, turning left along the farm road soon cross two bridges and, ignoring a track going right and a wooden stepped stile on the left, continue forward (now with hedges on both sides) to a point just before the entrance to the farm where in front of you is a line of conifer trees. Turn right in front of them to pass through the left hand of two gates. Now following the left hand hedge skirt the farm and its paddocks to follow the field edge to the top corner and go through a gate into a wood.

Crossing the old railway bed follow the sunken track forward for the short distance to a right bend. Here a narrow path, marked by a now faded white topped post, goes off to the left. Follow this path, with the occasionally white splashed tree trunk, to reach a wooden barrier. Here your path joins a bridleway where you continue forward on the same line now on a broader way. You are now walking through the mature oak woodland of Bell Coppice which is protected by the Nature Conservancy Council.

Arriving at the edge of the woodland you now join a track to follow it forward between field left and woodland right. This track will eventually bring you through a gate and onto the A4117 above the Horse and Jockey pub.

Go left along the road for a few yards and on the right is a gap in the hedge. Cross over the fence into the field and follow the left hand hedge up the slope into the top left hand corner. Pass through a gate and go half left to a house and then right with its fence to a corner. Going over a fence in the corner and straight across the field you will come to a fence/hedge and a gap into woodland. Go into the woods and steeply downhill, following a fence on the right, to cross a rail fence in a corner. Continue to follow the right hand fence down, then cross it and a gate onto a narrow lane.

It is possible, though unlikely, that this last short section through the steep woodland may be overgrown in high summer. Should this be the case then there is an alternative. Simply go left to pass a ruined caravan and go through a gap in the hedge corner to follow a broad track as it swings right through the woodland and descends to a gate onto the narrow lane. This is only a diversion however and should not be used if the right of way described above is passable.

Turn right along the lane – the attractive entrance to 'Tanners Bow' is to your left. At a junction turn left to follow the sign for Buckridge and at the next corner, immediately before 'The Highways',. there is a public footpath sign for Church Hill. Follow this as it becomes a broad green lane and a ridge walk to Teddon Farm. Here go forward with the farmhouse and buildings on your left to a gate at the end of a metal barn and below the track. Through the gate and forward down the field, with the hedge on your right, will bring you to a bridged stream. Cross over and go right to a telegraph pole in the field corner then left, with the ditch and hedge on your right, to the top corner of the field. Slightly to your left is a bar fence which you go over to now walk ahead across a field corner to a large oak tree in a hedge. Go forward with the hedge to a gate which you pass through to then go between barns to meet the farm drive right of the farmhouse. Here a right turn will bring you to a road.

At the road and immediately opposite is a gap in the trees leading into a hedged bridleway. Follow it for some way, enjoying the views across Shropshire, to then pass through two gates and follow the track left of farm buildings and through two more gates to arrive at a road.

Turn left along the tarmac road and then first left along another to join the B4202. Go straight across and along the 'No Through Road' to where the tarmac swings sharp right. Ahead is a signed bridle-path which you follow down to a stream — note the boundary stone marked 'RL' and 'ML'. Crossing over, follow the track up and out of the trees. Now keeping to the right, cross two fields and on leaving the second through a gate turn left along a track to pass Gybhouse Farm and reach the A456.

Go left along the road, passing a water tower, until opposite the drive to Moor Green Farm where there is a gate on your left. Go through the gate to follow the left hedge on a zigzag course. Arriving at a fence in the top corner cross it and continue forward, still with the hedge on your left, for about 75 yards to the second large tree where there is a gap in the hedge with an old gate across it. Pass through the gap and then proceed half right across the field towards a house and on meeting the hedge go left and through a gate into a narrow lane.

Turn right and walk down the hill to a right bend. Here you will see a fence stile directly ahead in the corner and next to a yellow hydrant sign. Cross it and walk the few yards to join a drive where you turn left. At a point just before the house you will see a stile on your left leading into a wood. Enter the wood and go up, half right, to a stile into a field. The path now crosses the field towards houses and to left of static caravans where it reaches a fence stile. Cross the stile to enter a hedged path and then join a drive to continue forward to meet the A4117.

A right turn along the road brings you back to the Plough Inn and journey's end.

12

Through Ancient Woodland

Clent Hills

Owned by the National Trust and managed by Hereford and Worcester County Council, the Clent Hills form a breathing space between urban sprawl and old rural Worcestershire. The walk explores Uffmoor Wood which has been tree covered since the last ice age, about 10,000 years ago! As long as can be remembered public access to the woods was prohibited until The Woodland Trust bought them a few years ago. Now their enlightened and refreshing attitude to access enables you to enjoy a delightful circular walk. There is a choice of starting points for this walk, Wychbury Hill or Nimmings Car Park, and the appropriate directions follow.

DISTANCE: 8½ miles
MAPS: Landranger (1:50,000) 139
Pathfinder (1:25,000) 953 & 933
PARKING: Roadside — Wychbury Hill; Car Parks — Uffmoor Wood, Walton Hill, Nimmings
PUBLIC TRANSPORT: Midland Red West services 192/292 (Birmingham/Kidderminster/Hereford) and 193 (Birmingham/The Walshes). Alight at The Badgers Sett and walk west along the A456 to pick up the route at the stile by Hagleyhill Farm on your left (see below).
START/FINISH: A456 at Wychbury Hill (GR 925814) or Nimmings Car Park (GR 939807).
If you are starting from the Nimmings car park then read from the point marked ➤ on the following page.

TARTING from Wychbury Hill walk east along the A456 to pass Hagleyhill Farm where in a few yards, and before The Badgers Sett motel, you will see a signed stile on your right. Cross it and follow the broad path across the field to another stile giving access onto a crossing track. Go left with the track and, as it swings right, go straight ahead with a hedge on your left and follow it all the way to the gateway into Hagley Wood.

In the wood turn right along a track rising through the trees to emerge into a pasture — the alternative that most people adopt is to continue

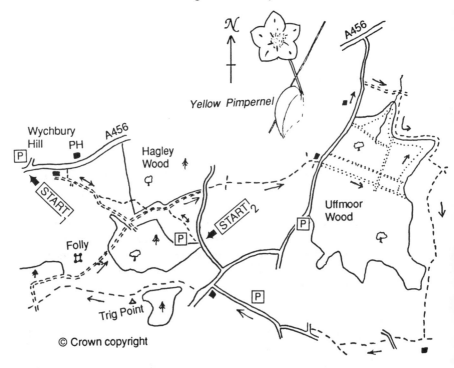

© Crown copyright

on the original farm track to then turn left and so arrive at this same point. Either way, swing left (or continue forward) to a gate and stile at the woodland corner. Go through the gate and forward along the woodland edged and fenced path to a lane. Now continue from the point marked ⮕ below.

⮕ From Nimmings, leave the car park down the steps at the side of the refreshment and information building. Go through the kissing gate and follow the path downhill to a stile left of a pond (which may be dry). Over this stile continue downhill — bearing slightly left — to another stile taking you into a wide fenced path. Turn right to follow the woodland edge to a lane.

⮕ Cross the lane and the fence opposite to continue forward with a hedge on your left to the field corner. Here there is a crossroad of paths and a substantial new stile left which leads downhill. Do not cross this but take the adjacent fence stile so as to continue contouring the hillside, still with the hedge on your left, to another fence stile. Over this continue forward, again with a hedge and fence on your left, to drop gently down and enter rough pasture.

Taking the right of three paths and keeping a hedge on your right soon arrive at a fence stile which you cross into a fenced path where a left and then right turn will bring you onto a wooden fenced farm road. Turn left along the road until meeting a white gate immediately before a house and Uffmoor Lane. To the right you will see a Right of Way sign, and so it is, but it's not the one you want! Instead you go through the gate and right of the house into the lane.

Directly opposite is a kissing gate into Uffmoor Wood. In the wood follow the broad avenue forward to a point a few feet short of the far perimeter where a broad path goes left. Go with it to meet the broad swathe of the Elan Valley Water Pipeline. To your right is a tempting stile, but stop!; it is not a right of way, and even though it leads to one and appears to be regularly used, you wouldn't want to trespass would you? Instead turn left along the pipeline to pass a low brick construction and then pass through a gate. In a few yards, and on the right, there is a lovely path through the trees — follow it. The path essentially follows a parallel course to the woodland edge and after a while turns left and, some distance further on, goes over a cross track to continue forward for some distance to then go left again and across two footbridges to meet another cross track. Here, to your right, you will see a gate and Uffmoor Lane.

Join the lane and turn right to pass Uffmoor Farm and then arrive at a stile on the right next to a drive gate. Cross the stile and follow the drive as it bends and crosses a gated stream bridge. Over the bridge turn sharp right with the yellow topped way-marker posts and follow the woodland edge. After crossing three stiles — look out for a large badger sett — the path arrives at a protruding woodland corner where again you turn right to follow the posts and the woodland edge. This will take you past a collapsing wooden barn to a stile which you cross to continue forward, for 20 yards or so, to another stile. Over this one you will enter a huge field where straight ahead and in the middle of the field you will see a marker post which is actually on the pipeline!

Arriving at the post continue forward on the same line and up the slope to a stile below an oak tree. Now simply follow the posts which mark the path and, passing a pipeline bridge over a ravine on your right, climb to a gate just before a farm. Take the stile on the right and in the second field head for the signed stile onto the lane just left of a white house.

At the lane go right and then immediately left over a stile to strike uphill for the gap in the far right corner of the field. Just left of the corner is a stile which you pass over and cross a field to a large upright post on an embankment. Turn right here and follow the hedge to a final stile and a lane. A left turn, followed by a right and then another right, will take you past the Walton Hill car park and to the T-junction at St. Kenelm's Pass.

Now follow the North Worcestershire Path arrows to the Four Stones on the hill top and then to the viewpoint just below the isolated clump of trees. Continue downhill with the way-marks to a fence and junction with a bridle track. Turn right following this track to pass the ruined sham castle. Bear left (although the track is marked 'Private. No Bridleway' this is still a public footpath) and skirt the edge of Hagley Park until reaching a junction of tracks.

If you started from Nimmings then go straight ahead into the field and follow the tractor marks to a gate and stile onto the fenced path. Immediately go right over another stile and back up the hill to the car park.

However, if you started from Wychbury Hill or the Badgers Sett go left at the junction of tracks and simply retrace your steps back to your starting point.

13

Scenic Salop

Church Stretton

This route traverses part of the Long Mynd, a ten mile ridge of open hills now owned by the National Trust. Its heath and moorland contains many prehistoric relics and offers the best open access walking in the Midlands. For this reason the paths are many and varied and often are little more than sheep or other animal tracks. The results can sometimes cause confusion so the ability to read a map and use a compass is important. Perhaps the most popular part of the Long Mynd is Cardingmill Valley and the walk, which should not be attempted in poor visibility, starts at the valley entrance.

DISTANCE: 8½ miles
MAPS: Landranger (1:50,000) 137
Pathfinder (1:25,000) 910
PARKING: First car park in Cardingmill Valley
PUBLIC TRANSPORT: British Rail, Church Stretton. Walk into the town centre and then go right, along the B4370, for about a quarter of a mile to reach a signed road on the left into the Cardingmill Valley.
START/FINISH: Cardingmill Valley (GR 449943)

IMMEDIATELY after the cattle grid into Cardingmill Valley there is a National Trust notice board on the left next to a wooden hut and parking area. If you park here leave the area and rejoin the road to go left for a little less than 100 yards where on the right you will see a narrow footpath — it can easily be missed — which goes right and up the hillside to a point above the cattle grid. Follow it and continue with it as it joins a fence, near houses, and then goes left with the fence to pass a house and meet a gate above the Golf Club House. Go through the gate and still following the fence arrive at a gated footbridge bearing a blue arrow indicating half left. In about 20 yards you will see a gap in the embankment on the left where there is also a mini cattle grid. Pass left through the gap, over the cattle grid, and up with a track through a shallow valley.

Ridges and Valleys

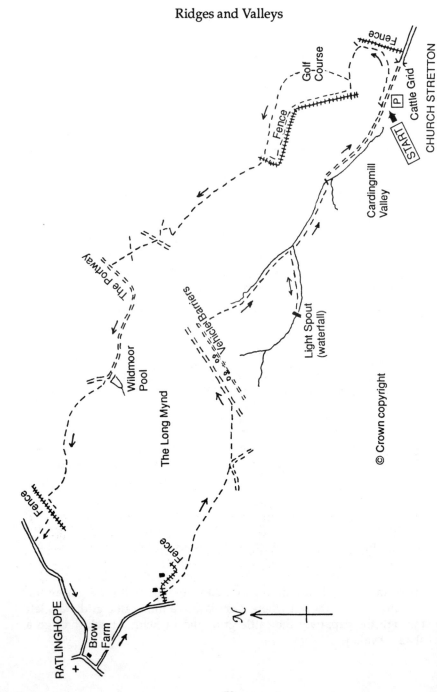

Soon passing a bell, continue with the track upwards and pass right of a white post to the top of a shoulder where ahead you will see the boundary fence of the golf course. Half right, and across a small valley, you will see a corrugated iron shed with a glazed wooden hut next to it. This is your next objective from where the right of way continues through the golf course.

If you are apprehensive of dodging golf balls then there is really no alternative but to follow the boundary fence — as shown on the sketch map — until rejoining the right of way at the end of the golf course.

However, it's not as bad as it might sound so follow the track as it swings right around the head of the small valley and then walk to the iron shed and wooden hut. From here initially head north, parallel to the boundary fence over to your left, and walk up through the ferns. To your right is a steep little valley. Pass left of the seventh hole (care! hole numbers can change!) and go up the slope just in sight of the boundary fence. Over the brow pass right of the twelfth hole and head for a black corrugated iron shed. Arriving at the shed pass left of it to walk half left on a bearing of 280 degrees to a wooden shed. Pass left of the shed and continue forward right of the thirteenth hole to meet the boundary fence. At the fence turn right and follow it to a white flag-pole (tenth hole) and continue with the fence to a wooden wicket gate in the corner, which you go through. This is where you can now test your navigation skills!

On the map the general direction of your path for the next mile is north-north-west. However it does twist and turn to achieve this so follow these directions:

Pass through the gate from the golf course onto the open moorland. Standing with your back to the gate, your path is ahead and slightly right, rising gradually above a valley on the right so as to contour Haddon Hill on the left. Initially the path heads north!

So, go forth on your path to rise through the fern and enjoy the outstanding views of Caer Caradoc, The Lawley and The Wrekin. Continue on the fairly clear path — but beware of sheep tracks — and ignore a path coming in from the right and going up left. A little further on you will descend slightly into a dip just above a patch of bog grass. Here the path continues quite clearly forward through the fern and now stays at this level for some way until starting to swing left above another valley named Long Batch. Soon you descend into the head of Long Batch to cross a small stream and swing right with the valley side to shortly cross a second stream and then in a while meet a third. Remember that in summer streams can dry up so you may be looking for a dry watercourse!

Do not cross the third stream, as the path does, but go left and up it to its watershed where just at the top of the crest you will see a track coming in from the right along a ridge. Join it and turn left to follow it for 150 yards to a broad, very clear cross track.

The Lawley

Go straight across to follow a bearing of 330 degrees up a slight slope on a poorly defined path — those sheep again! Very shortly you will meet yet another cross track (grassy) just before the final crest. Go straight across on your bearing and shortly reach the top where ahead you will see a stand of trees across a shallow dip that hides the Portway. Now simply walk the few yards down to meet this narrow metalled road. A short way to your right you will see a gated cattle grid and a National Trust sign — didn't you do well!

But if you find yourself at a well worn, but unmetalled, track you have come a bit too far north. So go left along this track to reach the cattle grid and N.T. sign.

An ancient trading route, the Portway was used by axe-traders in Neolithic times and, in the Middle Ages, by Welsh drovers taking their cattle to Shrewsbury market.

Turn left to now follow the unfenced road for three quarters of a mile to Wildmoor Pool, passing on the way a weather-beaten signpost pointing along the tarmac. Ahead are views of the Stiperstones on the distant ridge. Arriving at the pool the road passes between it and its overflow stream and then immediately bends right. On the left hand side, just past the bend, is a broad track with a marker post indicating Ratlinghope. Go left to follow the track through the heather and stay with it, ignoring a track left, as it becomes increasingly grassy and starts its descent to pass right of a solitary tree. As it broadens and descends further it meets an intake fence near a gate and the remains of a brick building.

Walk left to pass the gate and shortly arrive at a step stile in the fence. Cross over and walk down the centre of the field to a line of trees that lead you to a gate onto a lane. Turn left to follow the lane for three quarters of a mile into Ratlinghope — pronounced 'Ratchup'.

A tiny place, Ratlinghope contains the Parish Church of Saint Margaret and less than a handful of dwellings. Its quiet isolation is assured by narrow winding lanes and probably for this reason little has changed in the community. The church itself has an oak door with a carved inscription dating from 1625 and connections with the Scott family of Great Barr — now part of Birmingham.

Leaving the church continue along the lane and immediately pass Brow Farm and its Tea Room (summer months only) to then reach a junction just beyond. Here turn left up the lane signed for Belmore and Church Stretton and in about half a mile reach the gate and drive for Belmore Farm on the left, opposite a stand of conifer trees. Pass through the gate and turn immediately right to follow the right hand fence up to a point right of the house. This will bring you to the top corner and a gate which takes you out of the field to cross a track leading to the house. Now continue up and forward on the same line, now with a fence on your left, along a slightly sunken track.

Now on the open moorland continue following the fence to the point where it goes left. Leave the fence here and continue forward and up along a broad grassy track. Ignoring a crossing track, continue your gradual ascent of the hillside to the brow where a little way ahead and below you will see a narrow metalled strip of road. Walk down to join it on a bend at a marker post indicating the way to Cardingmill. Join the tarmac and follow it around the bend for about 40 yards to where a track leaves the bend on the left hand side. Follow the track, which soon narrows, as it rises through the heather to the crest — meandering a little near the top — where you will then meet a very clear crossing track.

Although you can't see the others yet, this is in fact the first of several parallel tracks all in close proximity.

Turning left follow this track to a point where you can see the other tracks and two sets of vehicle barrier posts on the right. Walk to the furthest set of posts and then go left with the track they border. Closely accompanied on the right by another track travel for a distance of some 400 yards where there is a wooden marker post to the right.

The post indicates various directions — you need the route that goes right and is signed for Cardingmill.

Following a broad track it begins its descent of Cardingmill Valley and then meets a watercourse left. Keep right of the stream and as the sides steepen follow the well trodden path down the valley. Your path, which initially progresses above the stream, is in fact a bridleway known as Mott's Road. In the distance you can see Church Stretton.

Arriving at a marker post and a junction with a stream from a valley on the right — Light Spout Hollow — turn right up this side valley and in about half a mile reach the bottom of Light Spout, a waterfall that cascades through a gap in the rock face. There is no defined path beyond the fall so you need to retrace your steps back to the junction of the streams and the marker post. Here cross the stream coming from the waterfall and take the lower (stream-side) of two paths down the valley.

With the merged stream on your left as you descend the valley, it slowly widens until the path brings you to a wooden footbridge at a car park. Cross over and follow the tarmac down to where it fords the stream. Here you stay on the left bank to cross two more footbridges and so rejoin the tarmac. Continue along the road to pass the National Trust buildings and then return to your starting point.

14

The Great Escape

Shifnal

There is a special area of Shropshire, bordered by South Staffordshire, which is full of surprises. Architecture, history and wildlife — all are contained within this walk.

DISTANCE: 9 miles
MAPS: Landranger (1:50,000) 127
Pathfinder (1:25,000) 890
PARKING: Shifnal
PUBLIC TRANSPORT: British Rail, Shifnal
START/FINISH: Shifnal (GR 746075)

STARTING from Shifnal parish church, head south west along the A4169 and just after leaving the built up area go left along a tarmac lane signed as a public footpath. Immediately after Mill Cottage, at a path sign, go right along a track as far as some farm buildings and, although the OS map shows the path as left of the buildings, go to the right and follow a reasonably well defined path, with a hedge on the right, down to the valley floor. Ahead, and climbing out of the valley, is the perimeter fence to the sewage works — not as bad as it sounds! — which you need to follow in an anti-clockwise direction to gain the road from the plant.

Go right with the road and, about fifteen yards after the fence on the left ends, go through a gap down through the trees on the left to a lower track. Go right here and just after the track starts to rise and to swing right take a good path to the left to reach a footbridge. Do not cross the bridge but stay on the same bank and follow it to the lane at Evelith Mill.

Charles II is reputed to have passed this way after his defeat at the Battle of Worcester. On his way from Tong, he was attempting to cross the River Severn and so make his escape through Wales. Alas, he was not able to cross the river and was forced to return to Boscobel House and the ignominious oak tree.

Ridges and Valleys

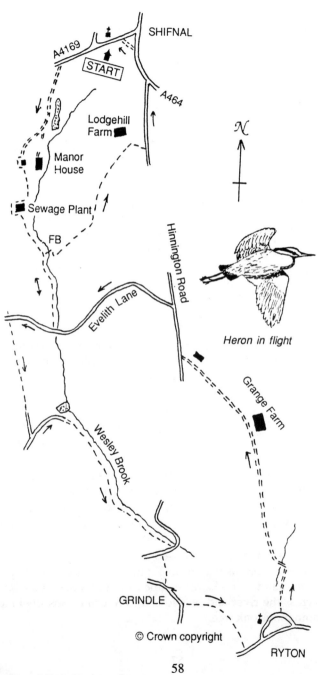

SHIFNAL

A4169

START

A464

Lodgehill Farm

Manor House

Sewage Plant

FB

Hinnington Road

Evelith Lane

Heron in flight

N

Grange Farm

Wesley Brook

GRINDLE

© Crown copyright

RYTON

Turn right along the lane and follow it for about 275 yds where, at the top of a rise, you will see a step stile on the right. On the opposite side of the lane you will see the entrances into two fields. Go left through the second gap and, keeping the hedge on your left, follow the field edge. Almost at the end of this large field you will meet a step stile which takes you into a short section of fenced path to enter a hedged green lane via another step stile.

Quickly meeting a T-junction with a narrow lane go left, through a gate, and follow the lane to the cottages at Kemberton Mill. Pass in front of the cottages and past two greenhouses to a stile into the field ahead. Go half right up the bank to another stile in the top right corner. The path now follows a series of stiles, above the tree level, until a steeply descending, then ascending, stepped path takes you through woodland. Continue forward, soon reaching more woodland through which an undulating path takes you to the bridge and road at Grindleforge where a fine sandstone ridge is seen across the valley.

Turn right along the road for about seventy yards and opposite a white house go up steps to cross a stile onto a path, over the hill, and down to the telephone kiosk at Grindle.

At the kiosk turn right, then immediately left and along the road to the last house where turn left through a hunter's gate into a field. Cross the field, keeping to the right hand hedge, to a stile overlooking a valley and directly opposite the tower of Ryton church. Go half right over the stile to drop down to the path and right onto the road before the bridge. Turn left and then walk along the lane which goes off on the left to reach the churchyard. This, being roughly half way, is a convenient place to take a break.

St. Andrews, Ryton, is a prominent eighteenth century church boasting a fine chancel and a beautiful East window, though the exterior fabric is in need of repair.

From the church continue along the lane to a signed path on the left, immediately after Church House. Follow this path keeping the wooden fence on your left to pass through a gate and then in a while left over the River Worfe. Follow the hedged track for the next mile and a quarter to Hinnington Road, the track becoming tarmacked after passing Grange Farm.

Turn right along Hinnington Road, then left along Evelith Lane — opposite a public footpath sign — to arrive, after about half a mile, at Wesley Brook again. Here retrace your footsteps on the western bank, as far as the first footbridge encountered on the outward journey but this time cross over. On the opposite bank go right a short way and then left at pigsties carrying a 'right of way' sign. Go upwards and around the right flank of Lodge Hill which at 374 feet offers fine views. What appears to be the remains of a ditch and dyke at the top suggests that the hill may have been a defensive position in days gone by.

Continue over a stile and follow the clear track as far as Lodgehill Farm where a sharp right hand turn takes you to the road. Left here to the A464 where another left turn will bring you near the centre of Shifnal. Opposite the Park House Hotel there is a footpath on the left which leads back to the parish church and journey's end.

15

Views of the Summits

Aston Munslow

Aston Munslow is one of the many villages that straddle the B4368, that long eighteen mile stretch of road running through Corvedale from Morville to Craven Arms. The village contains a fourteenth century manor, The White House, which has an agricultural museum and garden. The village pub, The White Swan, dates from 1350. As a boy, Dick Turpin is reputed to have lived in the village for a while.

This walk takes in the higher slopes of Corvedale, with views of the Clee Hills to the south, and the dramatic Wenlock Edge with its panorama of Caer Caradoc and the Long Mynd to the north. It's a landscape that constantly pulls and on a clear day you will readily understand its fascination.

N.B. If you wish to visit The White House and its garden please note that it is not open at all times. A notice on the gate states: 'The White House may be viewed strictly by prior appointment in writing with The Director of The Landmark Trust, Shottesbrooke, Maidenhead, Berks. SL6 3SW.'

DISTANCE: 9 miles
MAPS: Landranger (1:50,000) 137
Pathfinder (1:25,000) 931
PARKING: Roadside, and small lay-by on the B4368 just south-west of the village
START/FINISH: Aston Munslow (GR 512865)

IN Aston Munslow, take the signed No Through Road at the side of The White Swan pub and follow it to a crossroads. Keep with the same road, again signed No Through Road, to pass right of 'The White House' (*this is not the more obvious white timber framed building to the left*) and then rise north-west with it for a mile until reaching a T-junction with a track and, on the right, the gate for Little London Farm.

At the gate there is a bridleway sign pointing right and along the farm road. Follow it for about 250 yards to a bridleway sign and gate on the left giving access into a hedged track. Go left into the track and follow it up to a point at the edge of woodland where another track comes in

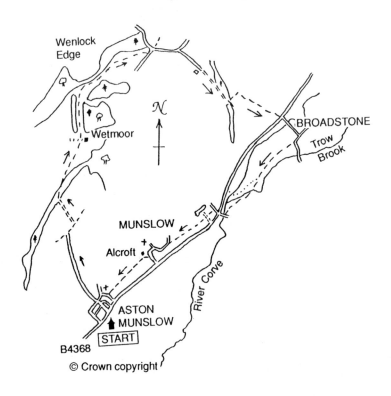

© Crown copyright

from the left. Continue forward on your track which quickly bears right and descends gradually down an escarpment. Soon your track joins a fence to then follow the bottom edge of the trees. Continue with the fence to and through a hunter's gate into a field. Still with the fence on your left descend the field to the bottom corner. Here go through another hunter's gate in the corner to join a sunken track.

Continue your line to now follow the avenue down to a gate which you go through to follow the right hand fence and so pass immediately left of Wetmoor Farm. Keeping the hedge on your right follow it to its protruding corner where just a few yards directly ahead is a gate onto a broad track which passes up through the conifers of Speller Coppice. Go through the gate and rise with the track until arriving at a gate at the top edge of the coppice.

Pass through this gate and in a few yards the one with an accompanying hunter's gate. Continue forward with a hedge on your right to the corner of the field where there is another gate with a hunter's

62

gate next to it. Go through to follow the broad track with a hedge right and trees left — you are now in fact at the top of Wenlock Edge, though the trees mostly obstruct the views here. In a while the track narrows a little but maintains its level progression until meeting an open area where you now have to leave the escarpment.

To your right is a very obvious hedged green lane which descends and which you follow. Passing in turn a white cottage, a tree house and then a much larger residence — all on the left — you will eventually arrive at a gate and so onto a metalled lane. Turn left along the lane to the sign posts at a sharp left bend.

Do not follow the signed bridleway ahead, instead turn right along the no through road signed for Stanway.

Walking along this minor road you will pass the lodge and left turn into Stanway Manor. Continuing forward with the road — and a B & B sign — in a while it swings right to then pass left of a bungalow. Ignoring a driveway right continue forward with the road as the tarmac ends and as it bends slightly left to become a hedged green lane.

Continue with the unsurfaced lane and follow it as it passes below woodland at the end of which it splits to go left and right. The left fork is the major and more clearly defined and is the one you follow between hedges. Soon arriving at a corner with two field gaps, one right and one ahead, you will see between them a hedged and sunken green lane going right and down. The lane is not your route, instead you go through the right hand gap to follow a broad track along the field boundary with the hedge of the sunken lane on your left. Your track now follows immediately parallel to the sunken lane for two fields as it slopes down to meet the B4368.

NB. At the time of writing the field boundary track is subject to a diversion proposal. It is simply proposed to move the Right of Way the few yards into the parallel sunken lane. Whichever of the two situations apply when you walk here, it should not present any problems as either way you need to turn right and walk down to the B4368.

At the B4368 cross over to follow the tarmac lane opposite signed for Holdgate. Soon swinging right cross the road bridge over a stream and follow it to a T-junction on a right bend. Go right, signed for Tugford and Rowe Lane (West), and in a very short distance where the lane bends sharply left you go straight ahead to follow the broad track that passes immediately right of Primrose Cottage. In a while pass two cottages on the left and then, further on, the restored 'The Goose House' immediately after which the track narrows appreciably.

Continuing along the now narrower track keep a look-out on the right for a stile with steps, you may possibly need it later. For the moment however, stay with the track to meet Trow Brook at a ford. The brook is most often fordable but should it be in spate, fear not — there is a more than acceptable alternative. (*For the alternative go to* ➡)

Having forded Trow Brook simply keep following the hedged track until arriving at a surfaced lane at Beambridge. Turn right and crossing a road bridge walk up to the crossroads on the B4368. Cross directly over into the opposite lane and follow it for 100 yards where, having passed a green electricity junction box left, you will see a stile up on the left. (*Now omit the next paragraph.*)

➡ If Trow Brook is not fordable retrace your steps along the track for 100 yards where you will see the stile mentioned earlier, now on your left of course. Cross it and in the field go half left to a stile in a fence just a few yards above Trow Brook. In the next field follow the edge of the brook for 100 yards from where, slightly right, you will see through a gap in trees the ornate buildings of Millichope Hall. To the left of the tree gap you will see a white footbridge over another stream — walk to it. Now cross over to the other bank where it is only a few yards to the gate ahead that gives access onto the B4368. Turn left along the road for the short distance to Beambridge crossroads where you turn right along the lane signed for Rushbury and Church Stretton. Follow it for 100 yards where, passing a green electricity junction box left, you will see a stile up on the left.

Before taking the stile it is worth going further along the road to view the unusual architecture of Millichope Hall and its attendant farm buildings.

Returning to the stile cross over it into an orchard where you walk forward up a slope and over the crest between trees. Below you will see a fenced drive leading to the Hall and in each fence a metal gate each with a kissing gate. Walk down and cross the drive to then cross to a stiled footbridge. Over the footbridge bear very slightly right up through the parkland to a metal fence and its protruding right corner which contains another kissing gate. Go through it and with the fence on your right head for the gable end of the house ahead.

Arriving in the field corner next to the houses, cross the fence stile into the service road and continue forward to a T-junction with a lane. Here go left and then down to a left bend at a junction. Go left with the bend — over a wall on your right is a church and its graveyard — to yet another left bend.

In the corner of this bend there is a field gate right and next to it a small wooden gate into the garden of 'Alcroft'. The public footpath and right of way goes through the garden gate and across the garden, but there is a diversion if you prefer.

(To follow the right of way continue from ➤*)*

For the diversion, continue around the bend and down the lane to a point just past the stone gate pillars and cattle grid for 'Alcroft'. Left is a white metal gate for 'The Miller House' and directly opposite is a small gap with a piece of yellow tape that takes you behind a wooden shed to a stile. This is the diversion — not properly signed at the time of writing.

Take the step up to go through the gap and then cross over the stile into a sloping field. Your path goes half right, initially following the left fence to its protruding corner and taped post, to then leave the post and proceed across the slope to a tree marked with tape at the top of the bank. Here follow the same line to another protruding fence corner with a ramshackle corrugated iron and wooden shed. (*Now omit the next paragraph.*)

➤   To follow the right of way go through the small wooden gate and cross the garden in front of the bungalow. There is a footbridge and stile, partly obscured by the opposite hedge, which you cross to continue up a sloping field to a protruding fence corner with a ramshackle corrugated iron and wooden shed.

Just beyond the protruding corner there is a stile. Cross this and walk forward, crossing a vehicle track, to follow the field edge upwards with a fence on your left. Just before the top corner you will arrive at a step stile in the left fence which you cross to continue up with the hedge now on your right. Pass through a gap into the next field and follow the same direction, still with the hedge on your right, to a step stile in the top corner.

Route finding is easy now. Just follow this same direction on what soon becomes an obvious and well trodden path across several fields and stiles for three quarters of a mile, parallel to the B4368. In the last field you can see a garage and filling station to the left and after crossing the field to a stile you join a narrow unmade lane. In the lane turn right and pass the tiny church down to a junction. Go left to the crossroads you negotiated at the start of the walk and here go left to the White Swan.

16

Malvern Hills and Dales

Eastnor

Not only are the Malvern Hills the best high level ridge walk in the Midlands but geologically they are amongst the most ancient in the country. This walk follows a major part of that ridge, couples it to an extensively landscaped deer park and joins it to some of the lesser frequented paths in this immensely popular area.

DISTANCE: 10 miles
MAPS: Landranger (1:50,000) 150
Pathfinder (1:25,000) 1018, 1041
PARKING: Eastnor Castle, Wynds Point, Quarry Picnic Area
PUBLIC TRANSPORT: (*Add 1 mile*) British Rail. Colwall station. (See box on page 68)
START/FINISH: Eastnor Castle (GR 733372) (or where convenient)

F ROM the A438 at the entrance to Eastnor Castle take the estate road opposite to go very soon through the barrier and over the cattle grid to then follow the permissive track — called the Ridgeway for about three miles. Look out for the deer in Eastnor Park.

The track is initially tarmacked but after passing a gate-house and crossing a cattle grid it becomes more roughly surfaced. Here, also, it enters attractive woodland — observe the numerous yews, more commonly met in old churchyards. Ignore any side tracks and on reaching the A449 cross the road very carefully and take the opposite stile down the sloping field and between the two stands of trees. At the bottom go left and then pick up the right hand tree lined fence and ditch for about 80 yards to a gate which you go through to follow the rising fenced track to a sharp left turn. Follow this north to, and through, a gated stile into an open field. Here walk half right to a field corner where a footbridge and stile await you. Cross over and, going forward, follow the right hand hedge boundary turning first left and then right to the next corner. From this corner go straight across the field to the gate ahead which takes you into a hedged track and then out to a tarmac lane.

A right turn along the lane for a short way will bring you to a public footpath sign where you go left along the drive to 'Spindrift' to reach the gate to the bungalow's double garage. Directly ahead is a distinct path that goes between the woodland edge and the garden fence, and so up to a stile. Cross the stile and continue upwards along the edge of the wood until reaching a wicket gate and stile on the right. (*Look out carefully for these. They are easy to miss!*) Go over and left to follow the fence up and

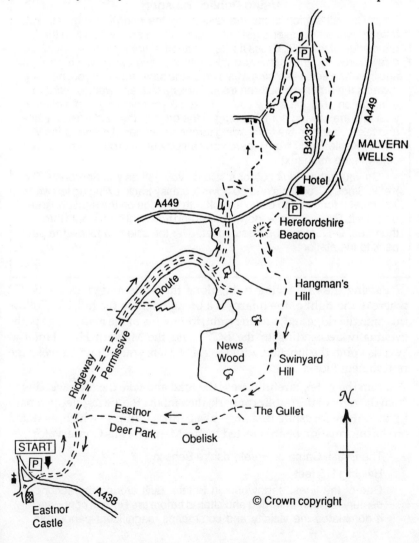

© Crown copyright

67

above a shallow valley, going through a kissing gate, to the head of the valley at the top left corner of the pasture.

At the head go right for a few yards to a stile. Cross this and go right, through the trees, to emerge at 'The Kettle Sings' café and restaurant on the edge of the Quarry Car Park.

Using Public Transport

From Colwall station cross the railway by the bridge and go straight forward into a field over a gate stile. Go half left and walk along the left hand edge of the field. Cross a stile into another field, go straight forward a few yards, up the slope and take either of two paths which go right and into the trees. Reaching a field go up the bank ahead of you, heading towards the rightmost of three trees. Cross a stile and walk forward with a hedge on your left and a row of trees on your right. Ignore a stile on your left, then swing right, keeping to the edge of the field. Cross a stile and take a track on the left leading through the trees. This will bring you to 'The Kettle Sings' from where you can pick up the route as described below in the main text.

On your return look out for a stile on your left as you approach 'The Kettle Sings'. Cross this and go down a grassy track, swinging left when you meet a fence to go down a track with a hedge on the right and trees on the left. Go over a stile, down the hill and turn right onto a path through the trees. On leaving the trees go left over the stile and follow the path back to the station.

Passing the café swing right, along the track, and cross the B4232 where to the right of the quarry is a broad track up the hillside. Follow this onto the ridge and, turning right, follow any of the many ridge paths eventually descending to the B4232 and the Malvern Hills Hotel at Wynds Point, the junction with the A449. Here you will find a welcome refreshment kiosk!

From the hotel, carefully cross the road and take the tarmacked way from the right of the public car park, then follow the zigzag stepped path up to the Herefordshire Beacon — alias British Camp — which, as stated on the information board erected by the Malvern Hills Conservators, is:

The British Camp or Herefordshire Beacon
Height 1115 feet
One of the finest earthworks in Britain. Built around the second century BC, later enlarged and altered before the Roman conquest, it dominates the vicinity and commands magnificent panoramic

views. Esteemed by John Evelyn the diarist to be one of the goodliest vistas in England.

The Red Earl's Dyke running along the crest of the hills was made by Gilbert de Clere, Earl of Gloucester, circa 1287, to mark the boundary between his territory and that of the Bishop of Hereford.

At a spring nearby William Langland the famous fourteenth century poet 'slombered in a sleping' and dreamt his "Vision of Piers Plowman".

Descend from the beacon and, reaching a direction marker, continue along the ridge for about 1¾ miles, heading to the top of Hangman's Hill and then Swinyard Hill. At this second summit look out for another direction marker (which is easy to miss) and from here go half right along the path for the Obelisk and Midsummer Hill and then go left along a woodland track to a broad junction of cross tracks. Go through the kissing gate on the right into the Eastnor Park estate where you are faced with four broad tracks. Yours is the third from the right and rises gradually. Arriving at the obelisk — erected by Lord Somers in memory of his son killed during the Peninsular War in 1812 — continue forward and down to cross the parkland. The path soon splits into several tracks — a result of motor trials. However, continue forward due east and, aiming between two pools, rise up to the Ridgeway.

If you started your walk from Colwall station turn right here, then continue reading from the second paragraph on p.66.

If you started from Eastnor Castle you are now on the track you used earlier. From here turn left and make your way back to the start.

17

Poppy Ridge

Blakedown

A ridge walk to lift the spirit and a village to tend the soul, both are featured on this walk! At the end of June many of the fields are ablaze with poppies.

DISTANCE: 10 miles
MAPS: Landranger (1:50,000) 139
Pathfinder (1:25,000) 953
PARKING: Roadside — Deansford Lane and Sandy Lane
PUBLIC TRANSPORT: Midland Red West services 192/292/193. Travelling *from* Birmingham alight at the third stop after 'The Old House at Home' (Deansford Lane — signed 'Bluntington'). Go back a few yards and go right along the lane, past Bissell Wood.
START/FINISH: Deansford Lane (GR 873772)

O N the left of Deansford Lane, as you come from the A456, is a public bridleway sign for Blakedown. The sign points generally towards a broad track heading in a north-easterly direction across a huge field and under power lines. Join this track opposite the entrance to Bissell Wood and follow it to pass just under the power lines where you need to take a cross path right. The path, which is on a line coming from the pylon to the left, is well trodden — unless the field has just been ploughed — and follows the straight line of what used to be a field boundary. So, having located it, turn right and follow the path heading for a stile and footpath sign in the distance.

Behind the stile and footpath sign is a gate which you go through to follow a track to a solitary oak tree near another gate and two waymarked stiles. Do not go through the second gate but instead go left between the oak tree and a right hand fence to walk up the slope to a stile at the corner of woodland. Go over the stile and forward with the edge of the wood and over a brow to then descend with the fenced path to the surfaced Sandy Lane.

Turning right along Sandy Lane follow it to the corner at Hunters Lodge and then go around the right hand bend for the few yards necessary to reach the bridleway sign on the left. Turn left with the sign

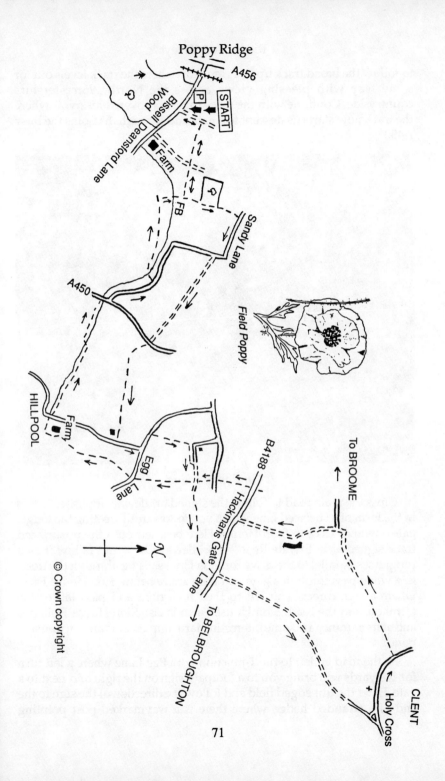

Poppy Ridge

A456

Bissell Wood

Deansford Lane

START

P

Farm

FB

Sandy Lane

A450

Field Poppy

HILLPOOL

Farm

Egg Lane

B4188

Hackmans Gate Lane

To BROOME

To BELBROUGHTON

CLENT

Holy Cross

N

© Crown copyright

71

to follow the broad track up to a ridge top where the track levels out for some way with pleasing views across the North Worcestershire countryside. Continue with the ridge to pass a covered reservoir where the track now starts its descent to a gate and through that joins the busy A450.

On Poppy Ridge

Cross the main road to follow the signed bridleway opposite. This is in the form of a surfaced lane which you follow until meeting the lodge, gateway and drive to Sion House. Here bear left onto the unsurfaced track signed as a 'Private Road — Bridleway Only' and follow it as it progresses parallel to the drive for Sion House visible through the trees. In a while pass through a gate and then arrive before Sion House Farm where a sign directs you left to then turn right and pass left of the farmhouse to the road. Sion House Farm is also Sion House Fisheries and at its entrance are some interesting farm implements and an unusual pond.

At the road go left to the T-junction with Egg Lane where a left turn for 100 yards will bring you to a footpath sign on the right and next to a gate. Enter the unhedged field and follow the direction of the sign to the end of a stranded hedge where there is a waymarked post pointing

72

ahead. With the hedge on your left follow the arrow to the field corner before Yieldingtree Farm. In the corner is a stile — do not cross it but instead go right with the hedge on your left and in front of the farmhouse to a gateway in the next corner. Pass left through the gateway and then immediately right to pass between a barn left and the hedge right.

Your way is now a hedged and fenced track which you follow forward to where the right hedge ends. Here the track swings right and here there are also several way-marks. Do not follow the track as it swings right but instead continue forward with the left hand hedge to immediately pass a stile and footpath sign. Note this spot for your return journey.

Staying with the left hand hedge will bring you to its protruding corner and a tall marker post. Here your way is across the centre of this large field on a heading of due east and aiming for the roof of the house seen in the far distance. Part-way across the field you will see a stile in the fence ahead which you duly cross. In the next field follow the same direction, walking roughly parallel to the upper right hand fence, and after a while you will arrive at a bottom fence and a stile. Take care not to drop down the sloping field too soon — stay with your bearing and you will arrive at the right place and the stile.

Cross the stile, followed by a footbridge, to another stile into a field. Here go straight across the field on a bearing of 50 degrees to arrive at a stile and gate onto Hackman's Gate Lane. On the opposite side of the lane is a signed bridleway for Clent. Enter this hedged way which you now follow for a little over a mile as far as Holy Cross. On the way you will pass a wind pump and cottage, a water treatment compound — from where the track is metalled — and then some cottages before arriving at the children's playground in Holy Cross. From here take either of the forks up to a road where you turn left to follow it through the village.

Keeping to this road you begin to leave the houses behind and arrive at a right bend. On this bend is the tiny and intriguing white Catholic Church of St. Oswald and St. Wulstan. Having the appearance of once being a barn it is partly timbered and, coincidentally, immediately next to Green Farm.

Continuing with the narrow road pass the large entrance gates to 'Pisces' and further on pass a footpath sign on the right. Soon after this you will meet a footpath sign on the left. Cross the stile at the side and follow the field boundary to a stile in the field corner.

Now follow two more fields on the same line and the same boundary to then enter a hedged green lane. Follow it forward and in a while left to pass in front of a house to a junction. Look for the amusing sign! A right turn here would take you into Broome village but today you need to go straight ahead along the surfaced farm road heading for Red Hall Farm. So follow the direction of the bridleway sign and in a while follow the road as it passes right of the farmhouse and its garden. Now passing 'The Park' and its tennis court soon reach Hackman's Gate Lane again.

Cross over to the other side of the road — it will be easier verge walking on that side — and turn right. In 200 yards you pass a gate on the left and in a further 80 yards there are some concrete steps down to a stile also on the left. In the past these steps were difficult to spot and it was always easy to walk straight past. Now there is a footpath sign to indicate them.

Over the stile enter a large field where the line of your path is across the centre. Stride out on a bearing of 190 degrees to the far side where in a while you will see a cottage ahead and a stile in the fence. Cross the stile and take the steps down to a footbridge to then walk up the opposite bank to join a track at the gable end of 'The End Cottage'. Go right and immediately left to pass between a rail and the front of the cottage — it is signed — to a stile. Cross over the stile and then immediately over a second to enter a sloping paddock where you walk up with the fence and hedge on your right to the top corner. Here cross the stile onto the path you used on the outward journey.

Directly ahead of you is the end of a hedge with a marker post and a yellow arrow. Walk the few yards to the post and follow the direction of the arrow forward, with the hedge on your left, now following a good field edge track.

Go through a gap into a second field and continue forward now with the hedge on your right. Before the end of this field your track becomes a hedge-side path still on the same heading. In the top corner of this field, on the right, there is a gate onto Egg Lane. In the lane turn right and then immediately left through a gate to follow the public footpath sign for Hillpool.

Through the gate follow the right hedge down and through a gap into a second field. Still keeping the hedge on your right walk to its protruding corner where you are faced with a field crossing. Follow the same direction along the lowest part of a dip and arrive at two gates in the fence ahead.

Here the Ordnance Survey Pathfinder Map shows the path going through the right hand gate and following the left hand fence — but it is wrong! The definitive map shows the path going through the left hand gate to follow the other side of the fence. So, following the definitive route, go through the left hand gate and walk forward with the fence on your right to then follow it left and right, keeping all the farm buildings on your right, to pass a gate and arrive at a stile in the field corner.

Go right, over the stile, and in ten yards left over another stile at the side of a gate to then descend to a drive before a brick wall. Turn right with the drive and follow it into the pleasant little hamlet of Hillpool arriving at a narrow road near a bridge.

Weir at Hillpool

Here turn right for a few yards to the footpath sign on the left that takes you along the side of 'Parkside' to then follow its garden fence and descend to an overflow footbridge. Over the footbridge — notice the weir on the left made of halved millstones — go right along the narrow pasture keeping the stream on your left. Continue in this direction for some way and then pass a dead tree with a sign 'Private Fishing'. Shortly afterwards the stream sweeps right to the bottom of an embankment. To keep the stream on your left involves following a path up the bank to a fence and to then follow the bank top past a wooden step — the sole remnant of a stile! — to soon cross the stile ahead and so descend to the stream again.

Still with the stream on your left in a short distance you will see a footbridge. On the other bank the temptation is to follow the stream side but in a few yards you must leave it to follow the path on the left up a slope to enter an old orchard at its top bank. Follow the top hedge through the orchard to a fence stile in the corner. Here cross into a second orchard and also follow the top edge of this one to the far corner where there is a step stile next to a gate. Cross it and go forward to the A450.

At the main road go right and quickly left along Sandy Lane. Passing Stanley's Farm Shop and 'Pick Your Own' establishment you will arrive at a double footpath sign pointing both right and left. Follow the left one down a sunken track to pass old farm implements and then at the bottom pass just left of a derelict brick building to then cross a culverted stream. On the other side you will see — right — what appears to be an old ivy covered mill. There is a stile in the fence near the 'mill' but do not cross it. Instead go up to a fence ahead where there is another fence stile and on the left a gate stating 'Private — No Access'. Turn right here to follow the now fenced track behind the 'old mill' and forward to where it then swings left uphill. Here you leave it to go directly ahead and right of a gate to a fence stile into a field.

Now follow the bottom of the field with a fence, trees and a stream right. You will now pass left of four power poles. At the fourth you will see a large pool on the right. A little way ahead is a short wooden section in the wire fence which you walk to. Next to it are the remains of a brick structure. Go right over the wooden section and forward a short distance to a footbridge. On the other side walk up to a fence stile into a field. A short way across the field is the oak tree and gated track you passed at the start of the walk.

Walk up to the oak tree where you cross the stile onto the track and then turn left to retrace your steps across the huge field and so back to Deansford Lane.

18

The W M 20 Challenge Walk

Wolverley

This last walk is a twenty mile elongated figure of eight I devised several years ago as a charity event organised by the West Midlands District Association of the Camping and Caravanning Club. It largely follows the Staffordshire/Worcestershire border and, despite its close proximity to the Midlands conurbation, is a totally rural walk enjoying hilltops, verdant canal-side, panoramic views, attractive villages and a stately home! In part it follows two long distance footpaths (the North Worcestershire Path and the West Midland Way) that run roughly parallel to each other and, by using available rights of way, connections are made to enable a continuous walk starting and ending at Wolverley, a charming Worcestershire village that straddles an impressive sandstone ridge. By using the public footpath that connects West Hagley to Stakenbridge and also the return loop from Wolverley to Caunsall, the route can be divided into three or more segments if you so wish. The section from Caunsall to the Standing Stones follows the North Worcestershire Path and as such is well waymarked.

So, why not rise to the challenge and raise funds for your favourite charity? 'Sponsored Walk' rucksack badges are available for groups and organisations. Please write to the publishers for details. (Meridian Books, 40 Hadzor Road, Oldbury, Warley, West Midlands B68 9LA)

DISTANCE: 20 miles (or can be broken into several shorter sections)
MAPS: Landranger (1:50,000) 138 & 139
Pathfinder (1:25,000) 953 & 933
PARKING: Roadside in Wolverley (limited), canal-side at Caunsall. Also Walton Hill, Clent and many other roadside spots on the route.
PUBLIC TRANSPORT: (1) Midland Red West service 5/5A from Kidderminster. Alight at Wolverley Sebright First School. Walk forward a few yards to the traffic island and turn right along the B4189, signed Stourbridge, to the Lock Inn.
(2) Midland Red West Services 192/292 (Birmingham - Hereford) or 193 (Birmingham - The Walshes). Alight at Hagley Forge. Pick up the route at the point marked ➤ on p.80.
START/FINISH: Wolverley (GR 831792)

STARTING from the Lock Inn, Wolverley follow the Staffs. and Worcester canal in a north-easterly direction for 2½ miles as far as bridge number 26 at Caunsall. (*N.B. At the time of writing the bridge number plate was missing — so watch out for bridge 25.*) Here leave the canal and turn right along the road to then cross the busy A449 and go over the signed stile to the left of the opposite junction. You are now on the North Worcestershire Path which will be followed to the Clent Hills.

Aim half left for the double stile and then follow the posts for three fields to reach the Fairy Glen. From here follow the sandy track ahead to pass the gate and stile for Iverley House Farm on the right. Continue with the sandy track to meet a tarmac lane where turn right to soon reach a surfaced

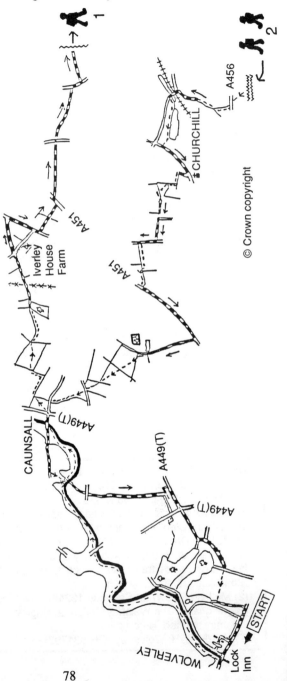

© Crown copyright

78

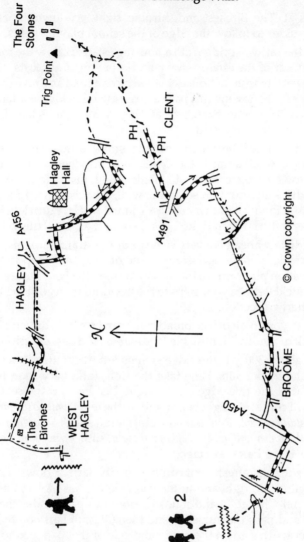

© Crown copyright

track on the left to then follow it to the A451.

Go left and then soon right at the footpath sign to follow the fenced path and in a while to cross another minor road and then follow the broad track to a T-junction with another broad track — the Roman Roads. Here turn right and then left into the surfaced road on the perimeter of West Hagley. Carry on along the road past the fine houses to a stile and sign on the left. Cross over the stile, walk up the slope to two stiles at 'The Birches' and, turning right, go downhill, changing boundary sides to follow the edge of the school playing fields.

Cross the railway bridge into a housing estate. Follow the road up to the top corner of the estate — way-marks are on lamp posts — and go along the path in front of houses to then cross a road and take the signed path opposite. Following this path across several fields eventually come out by the Telephone Exchange at Hagley and the A456. Take care crossing this very busy road.

➤ Take the road between the car showrooms and the shops (Bromsgrove Road) as far as the Lyttelton Arms where you turn left and walk up towards the entrance to Hagley Hall. Just before the entrance and at a drinking fountain set in the wall, take the fenced footpath on the right and follow it until meeting a T-junction. Here turn left, followed by another left, and then right to a stile onto the Clent Hills proper.

Immediately ahead is a very steep path. Go straight up this, ignoring crossing tracks, as far as an isolated stand of trees on the top and passing an observation platform. To the left can be seen the Four Stones — touch them for luck! Retrace your steps to the trees and then go along the ridge in a southerly direction.

Finding your path off the broad ridge can be a little difficult here due to the lack of readily identifiable landmarks. The best description is:

After about 300 yds the ridge swings left, then after about another 200 yds the track splits. Here take the right fork, very soon passing a bench seat at the tree edge on the right. Just beyond the seat the Hill Tavern will come into sight below and on the left. *If you go too far and pass right of a stand of Scots Pine near the end of the ridge don't be unduly concerned — the Hill Tavern will appear below, but right.* Either way you descend to it, for this is the half way stage!

After suitable refreshment continue on the tarmac down the hill to a road junction. Go right and immediately left along Violet Lane, signed Broome and Churchill, and follow it down to pass under the flyover. Turn left and pass the nurseries and then Oldmill Farm on the right to reach a footpath sign on the right hand side of the road next to a pair of houses. Go right with the sign, passing in front of a house, and then along an enclosed path into a field.

Go forward with the hedge on your left, then, at a gate halfway along the field edge, change sides and continue with the boundary on your right all the way to a minor road. Here turn right and then soon left onto a well signed and stiled path for three fields to then follow it as it becomes a hedged track swinging left in front of a house. Immediately after the house turn right along the narrow surfaced lane all the way into the village of Broome.

Just beyond Broome church, at a tree with a bench seat around it, is a road junction. Turn left here and where the road swings right, by the entrance to Hundred Acre Farm, take the signed path on the left leading over a footbridge and stile into a field. Go half right across the field to another stile and onto the A450. Almost opposite is a signed track to Harborough Hill. Follow this up, then go down through woods and cross straight over the middle of the field ahead, aiming for the house. At the hedge in front of the house turn right to a gate. Go through this and on a raised path between two depressions proceed to a large field.

The Clent Ridge

Go north-west across the centre of the field to the A456. Cross the road and take the signed footpath almost opposite to follow the edge of the field to a stile in the corner on the right. Cross the stile and follow the hedge to a gate beyond which the path becomes enclosed and leads you to the railway bridge near Stakenbridge.

Go under the bridge and then, just beyond the pools and the restored Stakenbridge Farm, take the signed path on the left just after a bend in the road. Follow this, below a house and past a large pool, until it comes out at a road — turn left here to the church at Churchill.

Opposite the church is another footpath sign from which you follow the surfaced drive behind the barn conversions to a gate and stile. Over the stile turn immediately left and go up to and over a fence stile. Go half right to the top of a steep but short rise and then turn left along the top to a gate and stile. Enter a hedged, unsurfaced lane and follow it to a T-junction and turn right. At the first of two adjacent gates on the left go through and follow the hedge on your right. At the end of this field cross over so that the hedge is now on your left and follow it to the A451. Using the pavement, turn left for approximately half a mile to a path sign for Caunsall. Go right through the gate and follow the track to a pool and Whitehouse Farm.

To the left of the pool there is a three-way footpath sign — ignore the temptation of a left turn here. Your path follows a depression ahead, left of the farmhouse, and up to a stile.

At the stile there is a signpost, but this can be misleading — it seems to be a moveable feast! Some years the trodden path tends to follow a route straight across the field to a prominent fence stile in the hedge ahead. *THIS IS NOT THE STILE YOU WANT.* It is simply a pipeline stile and if you cross it you will end up in the wrong field! There are in fact three stiles hereabouts. Two are close together in the north corner of the field — one, the pipeline stile, to the right; and one, a double stile, to the left. The stile that you want is the third which is further left along the north-west hedge. So, crossing this field, aim for the leftmost of the three stiles and for a point slightly to the left of Kinver church seen on the skyline.

On a similar line, cross the next two fields when you will see a stile in the fence next to a bungalow. This will take you immediately left of the bungalow and to a gap in the hedge and a minor road. Cross the road into the field opposite and aiming for the hedge ahead just left of the first oak tree walk across the field. On reaching the hedge follow it right to exit the field at another minor road. Here turn left down to the A449, cross this and then go forward over the canal bridge at Caunsall again.

This time go along the road almost to the Anchor Inn where you will see a public footpath sign and kissing gate on the left. Go through this past a small, young plantation crossing the meadow and the River Stour to the canal towpath. Go left here, over the canal bridge — number 24 — and up the rough lane past the static caravan site and across a minor road. Continue ahead first on a track and then a path at the rear of houses until reaching a path T-junction — go left and then right here to join the A449. Turn right along the road and then go through the 'castle gates' at Lea Castle.

Follow the sandy track forward, then left and right, to reach the entrance drive of the riding school and stables after about half a mile. Crossing the drive and the stile ahead go straight across the field opposite, aiming for a tree in front of the third house from the right. This brings you to another path where you turn left and follow a fence to the road. Turn right at the road — back to the Lock Inn

Index

Index

Also from Meridian

WATERSIDE WALKS in the MIDLANDS
by Birmingham Ramblers, edited by Peter Groves

The twenty-two walks in this book have been contributed by members of the Birmingham Branch of the Ramblers' Association. Ranging in distance from three to twelve miles, and covering the counties of Derbyshire, Shropshire, Staffordshire, Warwickshire, Worcestershire and the West Midlands, they feature brooks, streams, pools, rivers and canals in their many aspects.

ISBN 1 869922 09 3. £3.95. 112 pages. 28 photographs. 22 maps.

WATERSIDE WALKS in NORTH YORKSHIRE
by Ivan E Broadhead

Twenty walks in one of Britain's most beautiful counties and featuring brooks, streams, canals, waterfalls, lakes, rivers and the sea. From two to ten miles in distance, they include the areas of the Pennines, the Yorkshire Dales, the North Yorkshire Moors, and the East Coast and North Sea.

ISBN 1 869922 07 7. £3.95. 96 pages. 32 photographs. 20 maps.

BEYOND THE BARS
Ten Walks from York City Walls
by Ivan E Broadhead

Ten circular walks, from two to seven miles long and starting from the ten historic exits from the city walls of York. *Beyond the Bars* highlights the history, buildings, traditions and folklore of former villages now swallowed up by the city and encourages readers to explore and enjoy some of the delightful surrounding countryside.

ISBN 1 869922 05 0. £5.95. 192 pages. 84 photographs. 10 maps.

LET'S WALK
by Mark Linley

A book for those who wish to join the many thousands who regularly escape from the stresses and strains of modern life by rambling in the countryside, the hills and the mountains. *Let's Walk*, in its sixteen chapters, gives advice and information on clothing and equipment, walking companions, where to go, walking holidays, map and compass reading, wildlife in the countryside, leadership, difficulties and hazards, first aid, preserving the countryside, weather, and much else. As well as being an enthusiastic and experienced rambler the author is also a skilled artist, and the book is lavishly illustrated with over a hundred sketches and cartoons which greatly enhance the appeal of this valuable and informative guide.

ISBN 1 869922 03 4. £4.95. 144 Pages. Illustrated with 135 sketches and cartoons.

Local History

STREETWISE
Street names in and around Birmingham
by Vivian Bird

In this collection, based on the author's popular *Streetwise* column in the *Birmingham Evening Mail*, Vivian Bird explains the origins of many street names and shows their links with historical events, local personalities, great land-owning families, politics, industry and social affairs.

ISBN 1 869922 11 5. £3.95. 104 pages. 44 photographs.

Town and County Guides

WALKABOUT YORK: A guided tour through a historic city by Ivan E Broadhead. Second Edition. ISBN 1 869922 08 5. £1.95. 48 pages. 52 photographs. Map.

EXPLORING HARROGATE by Ivan E Broadhead. ISBN 0 906070 08 2. £1.95 44 pages. 31 photographs. Maps.

EXPLORING KNARESBOROUGH by Arnold Kellett. ISBN 0 906070 10 4. £1.95. 44 pages. 33 photographs. Maps.

EXPLORING BIRMINGHAM by Peter Groves. ISBN 1 869922 00 X. £1.95. 52 pages. 43 photographs. Map.

NORTHAMPTON: A guided tour by Tony Noble. ISBN 1 869922 06 9. £2.95. 64 pages. 34 photographs. 15 maps.

EXPLORING STRATFORD-UPON-AVON by Enid Colston. ISBN 1 869922 10 7. £2.25. 48 pages. 37 photographs. Map..

EXPLORING NORTHAMPTONSHIRE by Tony Noble. Second Edition. ISBN 1 869922 01 8. £4.95. 152 pages. 61 photographs. 24 maps.

Prices listed are correct at March 1992 and may be subject to revision.

All Meridian books are available from booksellers or can be obtained directly from the publishers. Please send your order to:

Meridian Books
40 Hadzor Road • Oldbury • Warley • West Midlands B68 9LA

Orders should be accompanied by the appropriate remittance, adding the following amounts for postage and packing: Order value up to £5.00 add 75p; over £5.00 add £1.00.

Please send s.a.e. for our full catalogue of books on walking, local and county guides, and local history.